# Royal
# Love Stories

## Margaret Nicholas

# Royal Love Stories

### Margaret Nicholas

Octopus Books

# Acknowledgments

With a book such as this the author must draw much of her information from previous works. It would be impossible to mention all of them but the author wishes to acknowledge in particular the following writers: The Duchess of Windsor: *The Heart Has Its Reasons* (Michael Joseph); Diana Mosley: *The Duchess of Windsor* (Sidgwick and Jackson); Frances Donaldson: *Edward VIII* (Weidenfeld and Nicolson); Richard Garrett: *Mrs Simpson* (Arthur Barker Ltd); J. Bryan and Charles J. V. Murphy: *The Windsor Story* (Granada Publishing Ltd); Steven Englund: *Princess Grace* (Orbis); Françoise de Bernardy: *Princes of Monaco* (Arthur Barker Ltd); Stanley Jackson: *Inside Monte Carlo* (W. H. Allen); Hope Cooke: *Time Change* (Simon and Schuster, New York); Peter Snow: *Hussein* (Barrie and Jenkins); David Duff: *Elizabeth of Glamis* (Methuen); Keith Middlemas: *George VI* (Weidenfeld and Nicolson); Anthony Holden: *The Queen Mother* (Sphere Books Ltd); Peter Lane: *The Queen Mother* (Robert Hale); Queen Frederica: *A Measure of Understanding* (Macmillan); William Hoffman: *Queen Juliana* (Angus and Robertson); Margaret Laing: *The Shah* (Sidgwick and Jackson); William H. Forbes: *The Fall of the Peacock Throne* (Harper and Row, New York); Farah, Shabanou of Iran: *My Thousand and One Days* (W. H. Allen); Christopher Warwick: *Princess Margaret* (Weidenfeld and Nicolson); Peter Townsend: *Time and Chance* (Collins); Graham and Heather Fisher: *Charles and Diana* (Robert Hale); Gordon Honeycombe: *Royal Wedding* (Michael Joseph); Hugo Vickers: *Debrett's Book of the Royal Wedding*.

The publishers would like to thank the following for providing the photographs in this book:
Camera Press 7, 61, 87, 149, 169, 177; Photo Source 47; Popperfoto 73, 10; Rex Features 121; Svenskt Pressfoto 139; Topham 29, 139 inset.
Cover Photography: Tim Graham above; Rex Features centre; Camera Press below.

Editor: Carolyn Bailey
Designer: Brazzle Atkins
Production Controller: Shane Lask

First Published 1987
by Octopus Books Ltd
59 Grosvenor Street
London W1
© 1987 Octopus Books Limited
ISBN 0 7064 2983 4
Printed in Great Britain

# Contents

Edward VIII and Wallis Simpson 7

Prince Rainier and Grace Kelly 29

The Prince of Wales and Lady Diana Spencer 47

King Hussein and Lisa Halaby 61

Princess Beatrix and Claus von Amsberg 73

King Constantine and Princess Anne-Marie 87

Princess Margaret and Peter Townsend 101

Crown Prince of Sikkim and Hope Cooke 121

Princess Margaretha and Robin Douglas-Home 139

The Duke of York and Lady Elizabeth Bowes Lyon 149

Juan Carlos of Spain and Princess Sophia 169

Shah of Iran and Farah Diba 177

# Edward VIII
## —AND—
# Wallis Simpson

The love affair that rocked the throne of England began one damp, foggy November day in 1930 at a weekend house-party at Melton Mowbray in Leicestershire. Nothing could have been more unpromising than that first meeting. Wallis Simpson was suffering from a streaming cold and had to take aspirin, while the Prince of Wales was fully occupied with his beautiful hostess, Lady Furness, and the prospect of good hunting. Finding themselves seated next to each other at lunch they talked about the desirability of central heating. Nevertheless, that meeting set in motion a train of events that changed the course of British history and gave the twentieth century its greatest love story.

At that time Wallis Simpson was known only to a small, élite circle of London society. American by birth, supremely elegant and charming, she was married to Ernest Simpson, son of a wealthy New York shipping agent who was looking after his father's interests in England. They had a luxurious flat in Bryanston Court and Wallis was becoming known as a hostess of some distinction. Though not conventionally beautiful, men were attracted to her and she had much vitality and gaiety.

Many of her friends in London were American. One autumn day in 1930 she had a telephone call from one of her special favourites, Consuelo Vanderbilt Thaw, wife of Benjamin Thaw, First Secretary at the American Embassy in London, and sister of Thelma Furness, whose name had been closely linked with that of the Prince of Wales for some time.

'Connie' Thaw said that she and her husband had been invited to spend the weekend at Burrough Court, the Furness's hunting lodge near Melton Mowbray. The Prince of Wales was expected to join the party. Unfortunately, something had cropped up at the Embassy and the Thaws were unable to go. Would Wallis and Ernest go instead?

At first Wallis said it was impossible. She realized she was being asked to take Connie's place as chaperone and though she was dying to meet the Prince, of whom she had heard constantly during her two years in London, she felt she would not know what to say to him as she had no interest whatsoever in hunting and no idea of the finer points of how to behave with royalty. However, Ernest Simpson was a fervent admirer of the British royal family and insisted they go. Wallis dutifully practised her curtsey and packed her new Molyneux tweeds for the occasion.

They arrived at Burrough Court at about five o'clock in the afternoon. A pea-soup fog had clamped down on the countryside. The lodge was spacious and comfortable, furnished in typical country-house style with mahogany furniture and pastel chintz covers. There was a blazing fire to welcome them and a low table drawn up in front of it laid with fresh-made scones and tempting cakes. Wallis, declining anything to eat, sipped hot lemon tea. She had developed a bad cold and was beginning to feel feverish. The royal guest had not yet arrived, so she went upstairs, drew the curtains and prayed that she would soon feel better.

At about seven o'clock there was the sound of cars on the drive at the front of the lodge, then a commotion in the hall. The Prince of Wales had arrived, accompanied by his brother, Prince George, who was going on to stay somewhere else in the district. Thelma Furness, her face aglow, brought forward the Simpsons and introduced them. Wallis made her curtsey. To her amusement, they went through the tea ritual all over again as the Prince had expressed his disappointment at missing it. He was wearing very loud checked tweeds and she was surprised to discover that he was not very tall. 'I remember thinking as I studied the Prince of Wales how much like his pictures he really was,' she wrote in her memoirs, 'the slightly wind-rumpled golden hair, the turned up nose and a strange, wistful, almost sad look about his eyes when his expression was in repose.' What attracted her most was his complete naturalness. She had expected to find him imposingly formal and reserved. His first impression on being introduced to the elegant, dark-haired American was to notice that she

8

had a bad cold. He also took note of the fact that she was not particularly interested in horses, hounds or hunting, but, during their brief discussion about central heating, he was amused to find that she actually *liked* cold houses.

It was six months before they met again. In mid-January 1931 the Prince left England for a long and exhausting tour of South America. When he returned in April, Lady Furness, who had been what the French tactfully call his *maîtresse en titre* for over a year, gave an afternoon reception to welcome him back. The Simpsons were invited. The Prince looked across towards them and asked Thelma Furness, 'Haven't I met that lady before?' pointing out Wallis in the crush. He crossed over to exchange a few words but was soon whisked away again.

The third time he saw her was in the splendour of the throne room at Buckingham Palace. In June of that year Wallis was one of several American women being presented to King George V and Queen Mary. From where he stood, behind his father's throne, the Prince watched her advance in her long, white dress worn with the traditional debutante's headdress of white plumes, ice-blue aquamarines glittering in a band round her head, an aquamarine cross on a fine gold chain round her neck. 'I was struck by the grace of her carriage and the natural dignity of her movements,' he wrote in his autobiography when he looked back to that day.

Immediately after the presentation Thelma Furness had a few friends in for drinks. Again she had invited the Simpsons and of course the Prince was there. He complimented Wallis on her appearance at court and admired her gown, then went on to talk to other people. After a brief stay he departed with his Assistant Comptroller and friend, Brigadier-General G. F. Trotter, saying that he was on his way to the country and already late. When the Simpsons took their leave, however, they were surprised to see the Prince and 'G', as he was known to his friends, still standing by the car deep in conversation. Catching sight of the Simpsons, the Prince hurried forward and offered them a lift home.

In the car he explained that he was on his way to his country home, Fort Belvedere, near Windsor Great Park. The place had been in a terrible state when he took it on, the garden a wilderness, but he was creating something there that gave him great joy. As he talked Wallis saw a sensitive side to his nature that she had not suspected, revealing, as she was to write later, 'a perceptive and imaginative spirit not ordinarily associated with the hard riding, nightclubbing Prince of Mayfair gossip'.

When they pulled up at Bryanston Court she asked if he would like to call in for a moment and have a 'nightcap' before continuing his journey. The Prince thanked her but declined. 'I'd very much like to see your flat one day. I'm told its charming,' he said before driving off into the night.

Though neither of them was to realize it until much later, 'the fuse that had been lit at Burrough Court had now begun to burn briskly', as J. Bryan and Charles Murphy put it in their authoritative book *The Windsor Story* and Wallis herself was to write of that June evening in 1931, 'That was how it all began.' Seven months were to elapse before they met again.

Wallis Simpson was thirty-four years old when she was introduced to the Prince of Wales. By then she had had a varied and not always easy life – indeed at certain times in her childhood and youth she had known what it was to be poor.

She came from a highly respected stratum of American society, both sides of her family being able to trace their descent from earliest colonial times. Her father, Teackle Wallis Warfield, belonged to a family that had arrived in America in 1662, settled in Maryland and produced generation after generation of successful businessmen, solid, puritanical and proud. One of them, Edwin Warfield, became Governor. Her mother, Alice Montague, came from Virginia where her family cut a dash as a handsome, easy-going, witty and worldly brood.

Born at Monterey Inn in the resort of Blue Ridge Summit, Pennsylvania on 19 June 1896, the future Duchess of Windsor was christened Bessie Wallis Warfield. She soon dropped the name 'Bessie' because, she said, it reminded her of cows. Her father died when he was only twenty-seven leaving his widow and baby daughter practically nothing. They were taken in by more affluent relatives and Wallis spent the first years of her life in a large, red-brick house on Preston Street, Baltimore. She was doted on and spoiled by the adults but had few friends of her own age and lived mostly in a world of make-believe.

The arrangement at Preston Street was not entirely satisfactory and when Wallis was six her mother decided to move out and take an apartment of her own. She supplemented her small income by sewing and catering but was hopeless at managing her finances. She had to be rescued by her sister, Mrs Merryman, the 'Aunt Bessie' who was to be very important to Wallis in the years to come. They lived for a time with her grandmother Warfield but their chief benefactor was Wallis's bachelor uncle, Solomon, a successful banker who paid school fees and other bills until Mrs Warfield married again. So the family made sure that Wallis was educated 'to be a lady'. She went to a smart day-school in Baltimore, then to Oldfields, a boarding-school which had the slogan 'Gentleness and Courtesy are Expected of the Girls at all Times' pinned to the door of every room.

By the time Wallis left Oldfields she had acquired a veneer of sophistication. She was not a beauty but her small, thin figure, perfect skin and smooth dark hair parted madonna-like in the centre gave a hint of the incredible *chic* she was to develop later. She was full of life, determined to have a good time and to marry well. She knew that this meant getting on in society. One of the first hurdles in Baltimore was to be invited to a Christmas ball called the Bachelors' Cotillion. She asked her cousin, Henry Warfield, to take her with him and made a superb entrance, wearing a stunning white satin dress with a white chiffon tunic bordered with pearls, carrying an armful of 'American Beauty' roses. She was an enormous success and discovered the heady delight of being the centre of attention. For the rest of her life she thrived on the social scene, never happier than when she was at some ball or reception.

There is no doubt that Wallis would have liked to have married one of the Baltimore élite, but when she was twenty she fell in love with someone from an entirely different world. In the spring of 1916 she had received an invitation from her cousin, Corinne, to visit her in Florida where her husband was commander of the U.S. Navy Air Station. Flying was then in its infancy and all airmen were regarded as heroes. Wallis had never seen an aeroplane before, never met a pilot, but the day after her arrival she was writing to her mother: 'I have just met the world's most fascinating aviator.' She had been introduced to twenty-seven-year-old Lieutenant Earl Winfield Spencer and was soon meeting him every day, finding a compelling attraction about this dashing airman. His photographs show a hard-looking man with little sensitivity but he had enough charm to win over Wallis's family

11

when he asked for her hand in marriage. Her mother warned her that she might find it difficult to fit into the restricted life of a naval officer's wife and to manage on his slender income but she was so happy to be wearing Win Spencer's diamond engagement ring, which had cost him several months' pay, that she didn't really listen to her.

They were married on 8 November 1916 at Christ Church, Baltimore, where Wallis had been confirmed. There was all the splendour of a full-dress naval wedding. Wallis wore a gown of white panne velvet, with a court train, over a petticoat of heirloom lace. Six bridesmaids attended her in dresses of orchid-coloured faille worn with wide sashes of French blue velvet. The church was filled with white lilies and chrysanthemums. Wallis was showing the world that if she was going to do a thing at all, she would do it in style.

During the short honeymoon at White Sulphur Springs, West Viginia, Wallis discovered an unpleasant fact. Win drank far too much and when drunk could become extremely aggressive and rude. She hardly touched alcohol and had never seen gin consumed in such quantities. Other problems emerged. When America declared war on Germany in 1917, instead of being sent to Europe on active service as he expected, Win was promoted and given a desk job as commander of a naval air station at Squantum, Massachusetts. He made such a good job of it that he was then ordered to California to organize a naval air station. Frustrated and moody, he began to take out his bitterness on Wallis. She tried hard to adapt herself to the life of a service wife, but her mother had been right: it did not suit her. She soon grew tired of furnishing a succession of small, temporary homes and filling in her time with golf or poker. She missed the social round. In California, where they had a Spanish bungalow set among trees in the semi-tropical town of San Diego, Win worked twelve hours a day. Wallis began to do her own cooking and give simple dinner parties, a chore she was later to turn into an art.

After the Armistice in 1918 Win Spencer was sent to the Navy Bureau of Aeronautics in Washington where he did nothing but sit in an office and draft reports. For a man who loved flying so much, it was like a death sentence. His drinking grew worse, and the cracks in the marriage became deeper. One Sunday afternoon, after a particularly bad session, he locked her in the bathroom of their apartment and fell into a drunken sleep on the sofa. After that she knew she had to leave him. Her family, shocked even by the suggestion of a separation, were appalled when she mentioned divorce. Her Uncle Solomon, who had been so fatherly towards her, roared, 'I won't let you bring this disgrace upon us,' and told her that ever since 1662, which was as far back as their records went, no Warfield had ever been divorced. She agreed to go back to Win and try again.

The couple managed to live together amicably for two weeks; then, one night Win just failed to come home. Wallis knew why. He had been too drunk. By the time he finally put in an appearance she had made up her mind to leave him whatever the family said. Win Spencer behaved rather well. 'Wallis,' he said, 'I've had it coming to me. If ever you change your mind, I'll still be around.' Later she wrote: 'Whatever his faults, he was still essentially a gentleman.' They had one more attempt at reconciliation when she was persuaded to join him in Hong Kong for a second honeymoon, but it was no use. The marriage had lasted on and off for eight years but now she wanted her freedom.

Wallis was twenty-eight when her marriage to Win ended and she went home to Baltimore to continue her social life. She made frequent shopping trips to New York where she stayed with Mary and Jacques Raffray, friends who had an apartment in Washington Square. On one of these visits she was introduced to Ernest Simpson. He was a quiet, cultured man of the world who loved books but also enjoyed dancing and going to the theatre. She learned that he was in shipping, working for his father's firm in New York. The Simpsons had only emigrated from England at the turn of the century, so when Ernest celebrated his twenty-first birthday on leaving Harvard he was given the choice of American or British citizenship. He chose British, having a certain nostalgia for the 'old country'. Wallis found herself immediately attracted to him and was delighted when she discovered the attraction was mutual. Ernest Simpson's own marriage had failed and Wallis was waiting for her divorce to come through – there was nothing to stop them except that, deep down, Wallis felt they were poles apart temperamentally.

Ernest had already been sent to London to take over his firm's office when she wrote to tell him that she accepted his proposal of marriage. His kindness and strong, dependable character won her over. He was overjoyed, and gave her a yellow Lagonda tourer, complete with chauffeur, for an engagement present. They were married at Chelsea Register Office on 21 July 1928. Ernest described the ceremony afterwards as 'a cold little job'.

After their honeymoon they took a furnished house in Berkeley Street for a year, where Wallis had the services of a butler, a cook, a housemaid and a chauffeur. She did not find it easy to build up a social circle. English people were more reserved than she expected and most of her friends during that early period were Americans living in London. When they moved to a new apartment in Bryanston Court, near Marble Arch, however, things began to look up. For one thing, she was able to throw her creative energies into decorating and furnishing, and created a home with a delightful atmosphere. She gave superb dinner parties and slowly built up a circle of interesting, amusing, rich people. Wallis Simpson, they began to realize, was a perfectionist with an exquisite taste in clothes, antiques and food.

The Simpsons had a fairly regular routine, playing bridge, going to the theatre and accepting numerous invitations to country-house parties. Then came that fateful day in November 1930 when they were persuaded to go to Melton Mowbray and meet the Prince of Wales.

Just then the heir to the throne was the most popular man in England. People who met him were charmed by his golden good looks and his easy, sympathetic manner. Wherever he went he was greeted by vast, cheering crowds. Though his leisure hours were usually spent with the rich and spoiled élite of the British aristocracy, he never failed when it came to meeting the ordinary man in the street. His obvious distress and compassion when he came face to face with the unemployed miners of South Wales endeared him to the whole country.

Edward was not as popular with his father, King George V, who found fault with nearly everything he did. Their relationship had never been an easy one. Though the King rejoiced as much as anyone when his heir was born on 23 June 1894, he was not the sort of father who could communicate with his children. Frances Donaldson, Edward's biographer, says that George V was oppressed by the necessity to inculcate in his children good character and seriousness of purpose. He was too often harsh and fault-finding, a martinet who reduced his children to a state of nerves in his presence. Edward could not even turn to his mother for warmth and affection. Queen Mary lacked the maternal streak and had an exceptionally reserved, cold temperament. Edward himself, speaking of his childhood, said that nothing would ever be as 'disconcerting to the spirit' as a message delivered by a palace footman saying that the King wished to see him in the library.

The Prince was an indifferent scholar and when the Great War broke out in 1914 immediately left Oxford to take a commission in the Grenadier Guards. He spent the next four years under fire with the Allied armies. 'How can I prove my fitness to be King unless I can hold up my head among my own generation?' he asked. After the war the King, seeing that his son's popularity could be put to good purpose, sent him on a series of exhausting world tours to cement Britain's bonds with the Empire. Everywhere he went he was given the sort of adulation that today is only accorded to pop stars. Women reached out to touch him, stole his handkerchiefs, ripped off his buttons. Men copied the clothes he wore and tried to fathom the secret of his style.

The war years and travel had shown him how to mix with all kinds and classes of men. He loved the freedom and hated the thought of returning to his father's staid court. Lord Mountbatten, who accompanied him on one occasion, said the Prince often got depressed on tour when he thought of the life that awaited him on his return. He would become moody and withdrawn. Mountbatten came to the conclusion that he was a lonely person, lonely and sad.

The Prince tried to change things when he returned home. 'He wanted to open the windows and let the frowst and fug blow out,' said Mountbatten. But his father saw his son's rebelliousness developing and soon had him on the carpet. 'Never forget who you are,' he reminded him. The King had no time for Edward's friends and thought his habit of going to nightclubs verging on the immoral, though His Majesty had never been in a nightclub in his life and thought everyone should be in bed by eleven. The more he protested the more Edward became determined to keep a private life for himself.

Many women fell in love with the Prince of Wales, but he, to his parents' dismay, seemed to be perpetually involved with other men's wives. He fell madly in love with the delightful Freda

Dudley Ward, whose husband was Vice Chamberlain of the Royal Household and Liberal M.P. for Southampton. People said Dudley Ward was too vague to know what was going on and, anyway, neglected his pretty young wife. The liaison lasted for years. Freda had two small daughters whom the Prince treated almost as though they were his own and he never seemed happier than when they were together. Perhaps the relationship with Freda became too cosy, too domestic. By the summer of 1929 Edward's name was being coupled with that of another married beauty, Thelma, Lady Furness, an American who had married into British society and was widely admired for her magnolia skin and raven-black hair. Lady Furness was not nearly as discreet as Freda Dudley Ward and during their affair his reputation was often in question. But Thelma had an extremely special role to play in the Prince's life and that was to introduce him to Wallis Simpson at Burrough Court.

At the end of January 1932 the Simpsons received an invitation to spend a weekend with the Prince of Wales at Fort Belvedere. They had not seen him for seven months, ever since that night he gave them a lift home to Bryanston Court. To be invited to the Fort was honour indeed, for it was the Prince's true home where he escaped the formality of the court and relaxed in his shirt sleeves. He had loved the place ever since he was a boy and could see its 'mock Gothic hodge-podge of towers and battle-ments' through the mists of Windsor Great Park. It was a kind of castellated folly that had been added to bit by bit over two centuries and used as a Grace and Favour residence. In 1929 the Fort fell vacant and the Prince asked his father if he could have it. The King demanded, 'Why do you want that queer old place? Those damn weekends, I suppose! Well, if you want it, its yours.'

The Fort had been so neglected it was almost a ruin and the garden a wilderness but the place seized Edward's imagination and he set about making it into a comfortable retreat with pictures by Canaletto in the drawing-room, central heating throughout, a bathroom attached to every bedroom and a swim-ming pool in the garden. The task of turning a forest of nettles and thistles into a beautiful garden became his great obsession.

Though Thelma Furness usually acted as his hostess at this time, the Prince received the Simpsons himself and showed them to their rooms. During the day he set Ernest to work with the other male guests, chopping back laurel bushes with a machete. Wallis was amused. She knew how Ernest hated physical exercise. After dinner they all danced to the gramophone and for the first time Wallis found herself in the arms of the Prince of Wales. She discovered he was a good dancer, deft, light on his feet and with a true sense of rhythm. She found him immensely attractive and he obviously enjoyed her company, but there was no sign yet that they would fall in love so fatally.

This was the first of many visits to the Fort in the next twelve months. When it became known that the Simpsons were so friendly with Edward they began to get invitations that would not otherwise have come their way. As far as snobbish London society was concerned, they had 'arrived'. On 19 June 1933, Wallis's thirty-seventh birthday, the Prince gave a party for her at Quaglino's and presented her with a rare orchid plant which, he warned her, would not bloom for a year.

Strangely enough, Thelma Furness and Wallis became close friends and often lunched together at Claridges or the Ritz. In January 1934 Lady Furness told Wallis she had decided to go home to America for a holiday. Before sailing she invited her to meet her for cocktails. Was there anything she could bring her from New York? Then impulsively she reached out to take her hand. 'I'm afraid the Prince is going to be lonely, Wallis. Won't you look after him for me?' Whatever the exact words, and they vary in different accounts, Wallis said she would certainly do her very best.

In spite of her promise, Wallis was not sure that she would be given an opportunity to see the Prince while Thelma was away. She was still not very sure of the exact nature and depth of their friendship. However, the Simpsons continued to be invited to the Fort most weekends and the Prince began to call at Bryanston Court at six o'clock in the evening when Wallis made a point of being 'At Home' to offer cocktails to any friends who might like to see her. He often lingered after other guests had gone. One evening he stayed so long she found herself forced to ask him, 'Sir, would you like to take pot luck with us?' The Prince jumped to his feet. 'Good Lord,' he exclaimed, 'I had no idea it was so late. I am terribly sorry.' Wallis went on, 'I know that beef stew is not very inspiring but, I can assure you, we have more than enough.' The Prince stayed, and it was the first of many such dinners. The Simpsons never knew when he was coming or how long he would stay, but Ernest, perhaps sensing something, would usually beg to be excused because of pressure of work and retire to his own room with his papers.

Lady Furness was in America from January to March 1934 and when she returned received such a cool greeting from the Prince of Wales that she suspected that Wallis had taken her request to look after him too literally. She even asked her whether the Prince was 'keen' on her, to which she laughingly replied that he might be fond of her, but in love – no. The truth was that Edward had been extremely angry to hear that while in America Thelma had been courted by Prince Aly Khan, who had a formidable reputation for snaring beautiful women. Aly had sent her red roses every day and finally, reluctant to let her go, booked a passage on the liner taking her back to England. Edward did not intend to let anyone like Aly, whom he detested, put him in danger of ridicule. When Thelma arrived at the Fort that week-end, she found a tight-lipped Prince and Wallis in command of the silver tea-pot. She sensed the closeness between them and with as much dignity as she could muster made her exit. Shortly afterwards she departed for America.

The turning point came one night soon after when the Prince asked the Simpsons to dine with him and some friends at the Dorchester. Wallis was seated on his left. He found himself for once talking freely and passionately about what he really believed his task as a Prince ought to be; his sympathy for the poor and his efforts to encourage the government and the bankers to provide better housing for the working class. This sort of talk would have been listened to with sycophancy and little understanding by the society people who usually surrounded him. Wallis was different. He realized her interest was genuine. She asked questions, gave him her own opinions, showed real sympathy. For the first time he felt he was being talked to as a real person, a man in his own right. She obviously penetrated his essential loneliness.

When he was Duke of Windsor he wrote in his memoirs, 'That was the start of my falling in love with her. She promised to bring into my life something that wasn't there. I was convinced that with her I would be a more creative and useful person.' Ernest Simpson obviously knew by this time that the friendship had entered a different phase but behaved then, as always, with great dignity.

In the summer of 1934 Edward took a house at Biarritz and invited the Simpsons to join him. Ernest declined, saying he had to make a business trip to New York. It was agreed that Wallis would go, with her Aunt Bessie from Baltimore as chaperone. They swam, sunbathed, played golf and obviously found great delight in each other's company. Sometimes in the evening they would dine alone in little candlelit bistros. Towards the end of August the house party swelled to nine and Lord Moyne of the Guinness family put into harbour in his yacht. He asked the Prince to accompany him on a cruise to the Mediterranean with as many of his party as cared to come. Aunt Bessie did not fancy a long sea voyage and said she would make her way home but Wallis, happy and excited, agreed to go on.

Though they encountered a force nine gale in the Bay of Biscay, the rest of the cruise was idyllic. They eventually anchored off Formentor, a beautiful beach on the island of Majorca, in those days an enchanted paradise. During the day they had picnics with champagne and caviar. At night Edward and Wallis would often sit alone on deck. 'Perhaps it was during those evenings off the Spanish coast', she wrote, 'that we crossed the line that marks the indefinable boundary between friendship and love.' One evening after dinner the Prince gave Wallis a small velvet case. Inside was a tiny emerald and diamond charm for her bracelet. Later he would give her enough jewels to fill Aladdin's cave, but this charm meant more to her than anything.

When they reached home again, Wallis showed the charm to Aunt Bessie, who looked at her shrewdly. 'Isn't the Prince rather taken with you?' she asked in her usual direct manner. Wallis replied, 'I would like to think he is truly fond of me,' then added defensively, 'I know what I'm doing.' Aunt Bessie, now over seventy and closer to Wallis than anybody, said quietly, 'Very well, have it your own way. But I tell you that wiser people than you have been carried away and I can see no happy outcome to the situation.'

After the Biarritz holiday Ernest Simpson began to perceive all too clearly what was happening. Wallis was drawn more and more intimately into the Prince's life and she entertained for him at Bryanston Court, serving delicious meals in an apartment filled with orchids and arum lilies. Ernest was absent more and more often on business trips to New York until one day, accidentally opening a letter addressed to him, she discovered that her husband had begun to seek consolation elsewhere.

News of his son's 'infatuation' with a divorced American had by now reached the King. He declared he was worried because this one seemed more serious than the others but he could not bring himself to discuss the matter with Edward. He sought instead the advice of his Prime Minister, Stanley Baldwin, to whom he made the statement, 'After I am dead the boy will ruin himself in twelve months.' Anxiety about his son and heir undoubtedly threw a shadow over the King's last days.

On Thursday, 16 January 1936 the Prince was out shooting in Windsor Great Park when a message came from Queen Mary urging him to make haste to Sandringham. The King, who had been ailing for some time, was now sinking fast. Edward flew to Norfolk in his private plane and was with the royal family on the morning of 20 January when the B.B.C. announced: 'The King's life is moving peacefully to its close.' By midnight he was dead.

Wallis's first thought was, 'What is going to happen to me now?' She had her answer within hours. The new King phoned her to say, 'It's all over, darling. I must see you. I'll break away as soon as I can.' But things had to change. If she had been conscious of an aura of glamour around him before, she now felt awed as the great weight of the British monarchy descended on his shoulders. For one thing, he was now addressed, even by those close to him, as 'Your Majesty' and referred to as 'His Majesty'. When he entered a room now she dropped into a deep curtsey. He invited her to watch the proclamation from an apartment in St James's Palace and afterwards she told him, 'This has made me realize how very different your life is going to be.' He reassured her, 'There will be a difference, but nothing can ever change my feelings towards you.' Then with a quick smile he was gone.

King Edward VIII began his reign with 'a good heart and high aspirations' and was busy from morning till night. With the coming of spring he started weekends at the Fort again, but the atmosphere was more formal and people were always rushing down from London to consult him on affairs of State. 'In the back of my mind,' Wallis wrote in *The Heart has its Reasons*, 'I had always known that the dream would have to end.'

When at last he told Wallis that he intended to marry her she gasped, 'They will never let you', but he reassured her that somehow he would manage it and that she was the only woman he wanted. Without her he could not possibly bear the burden of being King.

His first attempt to bring Wallis into contact with the powerful men who would affect his future was at a dinner party he gave at York House, his London home before he moved to Buckingham Palace. Stanley Baldwin, the Prime Minister, was among his guests. Baldwin was pleasant but distant towards Mrs Simpson. The occasion was to be the last that Wallis and Ernest attended together. They had discussed their dilemma privately and agreed that from now on they should live apart.

That summer the King announced that he did not intend to spend his holiday at Balmoral or Sandringham as his father and grandfather had done. He preferred the hot Mediterranean sun to the misty moors of Scotland or the flat acres of Norfolk. What is more, he intended to take Mrs Simpson with him. Edward chartered a yacht, the *Nahlin*, and cruised along the Dalmatian coast, through the Corinth Canal via Athens and Istanbul, escorted by two destroyers. Whenever he and Wallis left the rest of the party and went ashore they were met by wild crowds shouting, 'Long live the King!' and 'Long live love!' For the first time Wallis realized her private life was known to the whole world. Nearly every foreign newspaper seemed to carry an account of the cruise. In the French press she was described as 'the King's oxygen – he cannot live without her'. But in England the press was muzzled. The Establishment had come to an arrangement with the powerful press barons to keep the Edward–Wallis story out of the papers.

On their return, Wallis told the King that she intended to divorce Ernest and he arranged for her to see a lawyer who suggested that the case should be heard in a provincial town where it would attract minimal notice. She moved from Bryanston Court to a house in Cumberland Terrace. Soon she heard that her divorce case would be heard at Ipswich on 27 October and that the distinguished barrister Norman Birkett K.C. would represent her. Some friends drove her in their own car to take up residence in a cottage near Felixstowe and on the morning of the twenty-seventh the King's chauffeur, George Ladbrook, drove her into Ipswich. The whole thing was over in half an hour and she was whisked back to London with only a few people realizing what had happened.

In London the storm clouds leading to the great abdication crisis in November 1936 were already gathering. Baldwin had been to see the King at Fort Belvedere to try to persuade him to tell Wallis to drop the divorce case. Edward replied sharply that the divorce was no concern of his. If Mrs Simpson wished to divorce her husband, that was her affair. Baldwin emerged from the interview with a grim face.

It was on Friday, 13 November that the King received the famous letter from his private secretary, Alexander Harding, warning him that the press could not be silenced much longer and when the dam burst the effect would be 'calamitous'. The Government, he said, might well resign and he had 'reason to know' that the King would find it impossible to find anybody to form a new one. He ended the letter by pointing out that they were all sitting on a time-bomb and that Mrs Simpson should go abroad without further delay.

After reading this letter, the King sent for his old friend the barrister Walter Monckton to act as his personal adviser. 'If the government is opposed to our marriage, then I am prepared to go,' he told him.

For Wallis life had become a nightmare. People gathered to watch her in the street, vulgar rhymes were circulating about her and every post brought abusive letters. Matters reached a climax when Scotland Yard heard of a plan to blow up her house. 'I began to feel like a hunted animal,' she wrote. The King decided she would be safer at Fort Belvedere.

On Wednesday, 2 December the King drove to London for a meeting with Baldwin. He had been given the ultimatum. He could either renounce Wallis and remain King or he could abdicate and hand over the crown to his brother, the Duke of York. 'I don't', he told Wallis, 'intend to give you up.'

She now realized fully and painfully that their love had brought them to the edge of a terrible chasm. Through her the throne of England was in danger. She knew she had to leave immediately. Only then was there a slight chance of the crisis being defused.

The only place she felt she would be safe was at the home of her old friends Herman and Katherine Rogers near Cannes. When she phoned, asking for their help, they did not hesitate. 'Yes, come at once,' they urged her. Edward decided that his Lord-in-Waiting, Lord Brownlow, a man of absolute integrity, should go with her. He arrived at the Fort just as it was getting dark, bringing Inspector Evans of Scotland Yard who had also been detailed to go with them. Wallis felt numb, realizing that there was a chance that she might never see Edward again. She crouched low on the back seat and the car sped away. The newspapermen waiting along the roads outside Fort Belvedere had no idea that Wallis was on her way to France.

They drove to Newhaven where Wallis's Buick had already been shipped aboard the ferry and two cabins reserved for Mr and Mrs Harris. On the other side began a nightmare journey in which they avoided all the main routes and wound their way through hundreds of little towns and villages. Reporters seemed to be waiting at every turn. At one point Wallis phoned the King but the line was so bad neither could hear what the other said. It took them three days to reach the Rogers' Villa Lou Viei near Cannes. They drove though the gates with Wallis crouched on the floor under a rug, and she collapsed into her friends' arms, miserable and exhausted.

Six days later on 10 December 1936, Edward VIII gave up the throne of England. It was decided he would assume the title Duke of Windsor. Though his mother, Queen Mary, felt he should save himself the emotional strain of addressing the nation and that Prime Minister Baldwin had said all there was to be said, Edward insisted on broadcasting his own personal farewell to the people of Britain.

From a small room in Windsor Castle the former King made his historic farewell, which was both moving and dramatic. Millions, gathered round their wireless sets, listened with tears in their eyes. His voice was calm as he told them: 'I have found it impossible to carry the heavy burden of responsibility and to discharge my duties as King as I would wish without the help and support of the woman I love.' He stressed, 'The other person most concerned has tried up to the last to persuade me to take a different course,' and finally he ended, 'God bless you all. God save the King'.

All that was left for him to do was to say goodbye to his family at Royal Lodge. At about eleven o'clock that night he was driven to Portsmouth where he embarked on H.M.S. *Fury* and set sail for the Continent and his sanctuary at Schloss Enzesfeld in Austria.

The Duke did not see Wallis again for some weeks but they spoke to each other every night on the telephone. For one thing, her divorce had to go through its final stage; and the Duke was anxious that nothing should mar or interfere with his brother's coronation on 12 May. The wedding was eventually fixed for 3 June 1937 and both Wallis and the Duke were happy enough for it to take place in France, where strict laws about the privacy of individuals would protect them from sightseers and journalists. When a French-American, Charles Bedaux, offered to lend them his château near Tours, they accepted. The Château de Candé was set in the middle of a park and would be ideal.

Wallis chose a small salon with pale panelled walls and Louis XVI furniture for the wedding ceremony and spent her days planning everything down to the last detail. She insisted until the last moment that this was a marriage she never intended to take place. She had never meant to come between the man she loved and his Crown. But now it had happened she was going to do everything in her power to make him happy.

The weather was glorious on the day of their wedding. The Duke's friend and former aide 'Fruity' Metcalfe arrived to be best man and Walter Monckton was among the eight guests. Wallis looked superb in a long, simple dress of pale-blue crêpe satin with a matching hat, the Duke's wedding present, a diamond and sapphire bracelet, glittering on her wrist. He was boyishly handsome. Anyone could see they were deeply in love.

Count Munster put his castle at their disposal for three months and for that short time they shut out the world and all its problems, blissfully happy that they were together at last.

Wallis had sworn that she would spend the rest of her life trying to make Edward's sacrifice worth while and most people believe she did. She made beautiful homes for him in France, entertained with vivacity and skill and kept her elegant good looks. He adored her until the end and she made it clear that he was the most important thing in her life. The Duke was angry that his Duchess was never given royal status and the quarrel over this matter kept him apart from his family for years. He always called her 'darling' or 'sweetheart' but insisted that on formal occasions she should be referred to as Her Royal Highness.

For years they seemed to be always on the move, appearing at all the smart places in great style but rootless. They spent the war years in the Bahamas where the Duke for once had a definite job in his role of governor. But he was only allowed to function as a figurehead. The late Forties and Fifties were notable for the number of balls, galas and parties they attended on one side of the Atlantic or the other, for ever travelling with mountains of luggage. The Duke still cherished hopes of returning to England but Wallis preferred France.

Their first home together was a large white house with green shutters near the sea at Cap d'Antibes. They moved into the Château de la Croe during the summer of 1938, filling the rooms with some of the treasures that the Duke had had sent out to him, but it was only a temporary haven. The Duchess never liked to be away from the centre of things for long and in winter they moved into their Paris house where Wallis gave legendary parties in the magnificent drawing-rooms decorated to perfection with antique furniture, silver, rare porcelain and great bowls of hothouse flowers. When guests arrived for dinner they were received by footmen in scarlet livery and the table would be set, as if for a royal banquet, with finest crystal and silver and golden goblets filled with white arum lilies. Wallis had always said she wanted the Duke to live just like a king. He was only happy when he was with her. If she went away he pined and counted the days to her return.

They usually stayed in France from April until after Christmas, when they went to America, staying at the Waldorf Tower in New York where they rented a luxurious apartment with a spectacular view. From there they might go on to Palm Beach to stay with friends or to Baltimore where Wallis was received like a queen.

In the Fifties they found the house that brought them their greatest happiness and contentment. It was a picturesque seventeenth-century mill belonging to the painter Drian, only forty-five minutes' drive from Paris, near Gif sur Yvette in the Vallée de Chevreuse. They fell in love with it the moment they saw it and the painter was willing to sell. Standing beside a rushing mill-stream, it had a cobbled courtyard, out-houses and barns, and a wilderness of a garden. Wallis used all her skill to turn it into an enchanting home. The garden proved to be just the challenge the Duke had been waiting for. He proceeded to create a little piece of England with herbaceous borders, perfect lawns, and magical rock gardens with little waterfalls splashing among rare alpine plants.

As the years went by, however, people began to wonder why the Windsors had been shut out so long from England; why the rift caused by the abdication had not healed; why Edward had not been able to take his Duchess home to England. The healing touch came almost too late, but it was significant. The Duke had been a heavy smoker all his life and, though Wallis tried to persuade him to give it up, it was the one sphere in which she seemed to have no influence. Towards the end of 1971 it was found he had cancer of the throat. The following May, when Queen Elizabeth went to Paris on a state visit, she called to see the Windsors at their house in the Bois de Boulogne. Though the Duke was frail, ill and not far from death, he fully understood what the visit meant. At the end he was at last being taken back into the fold. The Queen had tea with Wallis, then left.

The Duke of Windsor died on 28 May 1972. When his body was taken home to England sixty thousand people filed past his coffin to pay homage to the golden-haired King they once knew. The Queen sent one of her private planes to bring the Duchess to England for his funeral. She never got over his death. To her the idea of life without him was impossible. Just over a year after his funeral the Duchess let it be known that she would like to visit the Duke's grave at Frogmore on the anniversary of his birthday – 23 June. Things were set in motion immediately to fulfil her wish. The Queen sent a plane to fetch her and Lord Mountbatten and the Duke of Kent were waiting to meet her at the airport when she flew in from Paris. She laid flowers on his grave and stood alone with her memories for quite a while. The Queen invited her to tea, then she flew back to France without a backward glance. The future must have seemed curiously empty for her.

Her health was beginning to fail. She withdrew more and more into the sanctuary of the house they had shared, giving orders that the Duke's room was to be left exactly as it had been when he was still alive, with his suits hanging in the cupboard, his shirts stacked in the drawers, his brushes and combs set out on the dressing-table. Every night she would go to his room before retiring to call out 'Good night, David.' She died on 25 April 1986 and a promise was kept. She was brought back to England to lie beside Edward for ever in the royal mausolem at Frogmore.

# Prince Rainier
## —AND—
# Grace Kelly

**B**efore she ever set foot in a place called Monaco, Grace Kelly was considered the nearest thing Hollywood had to a real, live princess. She was cool, elegant, serene, and had an abundance of what her producers called 'class'. When, therefore, it was announced on 5 January 1956 that the M.G.M. star was to marry Prince Rainier, a descendant of one of Europe's oldest aristocratic families, most people believed she had at last found the role for which she was truly destined.

Gossip writers had been watching her for years, coupling her name with some of the most famous leading men in the world. Many of her co-stars did fall in love with her but she kept her ice-cool image and steered her way through the Hollywood jungle like the well-brought-up Catholic girl she really was. By the time she was twenty-five and at the height of her fame she was beginning to feel she would never ever find the right man. He was, in fact, waiting for her in a palace far away on the other side of the Atlantic.

Grace and Prince Rainier of Monaco might never have met if someone had not persuaded her to attend the Cannes Film Festival and represent the American film community in the spring of 1955. She did not want to go. For one thing she was about to start filming *High Society* with Bing Crosby and Frank Sinatra. She was also busy changing apartments in New York and was at a difficult time in an affair with couturier Oleg Cassini, who was trying to sweep her off her feet. At last she agreed, having been convinced that a trip to the French Riviera would be relaxing and set her up for the months of filming ahead.

Cannes at Festival time was thick with stars, but Grace Kelly with her corn-gold hair, patrician features and cool elegance seemed to move in a galaxy of her own. One night Elsa Maxwell, the society hostess, asked her to join a dinner-party which included Van Johnson, Charles Boyer, Olivia de Havilland and her husband, Pierre Gallante, then a director of *Paris Match*, who was fascinated by the star and her beauty. They had met before and he had told her he would like to do a picture story on her for *Match* and combine it with a feature on Monaco, the Principality next door to Cannes with its famous casino at Monte Carlo. That night he confirmed their plans. Prince Rainier had agreed to show them round his palace and its gardens and to be photographed with Miss Kelly.

On the afternoon of 6 May Grace walked into the palace at Monaco for the first time. It was blazing hot and the old stone walls glowed yellow in the fierce sunlight. She had chosen to wear a blue and white flowered dress with full, flounced skirts which showed off her tiny waist. Her silky blonde hair was drawn back into a chignon covered with tiny white flowers. The Prince was a little late and as the party waited in a reception room she toyed nervously with her white gloves.

When Prince Rainier entered the room she found herself face to face with a short, stocky, dark-haired aristocrat whose rather sullen good looks were transformed by a quick, charming smile. She bent her knee in a quick American curtsey and shook hands. In a disarming, shy manner he apologized for keeping everybody waiting and asked Grace if she would like to accompany him through the palace.

Together they strolled from room to room, then out on to the ramparts which gave a view of the whole Principality, including the harbour. Cameras clicking around them, they walked on through the gardens. Rainier asked if the film party would like to see his small zoo and with evident pride he led the way towards a cage which held two magnificent Sumatra tigers only recently arrived from the Far East. Grace was startled when he put his arm through the bars of the cage and began to scratch one of them behind the ears, playfully ruffling its coat and calling it by name. She could see that he had tremendous rapport with the animals and admired the way he approached them without fear, any shyness disappearing as he talked about their habits.

They walked on, quietly talking together until they reached the tropical gardens. It was noticed by those present that by the end of the visit they had become absorbed in each other, rather serious and thoughtful. The whole thing was over in under an hour. They did not even have time for the tea that had been laid on for them at the palace – as Grace had an important meeting to attend in Cannes. The party took its leave. Grace was subdued on the way back, only saying in answer to Gallante's questions: 'He is charming. Very, very charming.'

She wrote a cordial thank you letter to which Prince Rainier replied warmly but formally. There was nothing more on either side to indicate that they would ever meet again.

The Prince had, of course, seen Grace Kelly on the screen many times and had admired her. But at that encounter in Monaco she had seemed to him very different from any of the other screen goddesses he had come into contact with. She was different and her background had a great deal to do with it.

She was born into a big, energetic Irish family in Philadelphia in 1929. Her father, Jack Kelly, the son of an immigrant from County Mayo, had started life as a bricklayer and made a fortune in the construction business. His great pride was the fact that he had won an Olympic medal for sculling in his salad days. Her mother, Margaret, a former fashion model, had become the first woman physical education instructor at the University of Pennsylvania. The only things that mattered if you were a Kelly was to *achieve* something and to be true to the Catholic faith.

Grace was the quiet one of the family. She was brought up in the handsome, neo-Georgian house the Kellys owned in the smartest part of Philadelphia, then went to an academy run by nuns before finishing her education at an exclusive girls' school. She took part in plenty of amateur dramatics and at an early age decided she wanted to make acting her profession. The family was not too pleased. Grace's mother considered actors somewhat 'shallow' and did not like their lifestyle. The only connection the Kellys had had with the theatre before was through one uncle who had played in vaudeville and another who had written a Pulitzer-prize-winning play none of them had ever seen. At seventeen, however, Grace headed for New York and the American Academy of Dramatic Art.

She was already a very cool and self-possessed beauty and

earned her keep by modelling in advertisements for toothpaste and beer. She could have made a fortune as a model but the idea did not appeal to her. When she had finished at drama school she preferred to take any jobs offered to her in stock companies until a Broadway producer gave her the part of Raymond Massey's daughter in Strindberg's *The Father*. Though her performance did not set any lamps alight as far as the critics were concerned, her looks and her poise caught the eye of a Hollywood scout and she was offered a screen test. The 'rushes' were disappointing. She did not seem to generate any feeling on screen. On the strength of her looks, however, she was given a part in a low-budget thriller.

Her breakthrough came playing opposite Gary Cooper in the classic Western *High Noon*. His personality seemed to bring out her own star quality and M.G.M. quickly offered her a seven-year contract. Within five years she made eleven films, working with leading men including Clark Gable, James Stewart, Ray Milland, Bing Crosby and Cary Grant, and slowly established her position as 'first lady' of Hollywood.

The film that probably made her a star was the jungle romance *Mogambo* with Clark Gable in 1952. Gable came close to assessing her appeal when he said 'her cool looks seem to hide a promise of smouldering sexuality and every man thinks he could be the one to light the flame'. Steven Englund in his biography of Grace Kelly says that working on *Mogambo* she obviously fell just a little bit in love with Gable but their relationship was really one of friendship. She remained very fond of him and he of her.

After *Mogambo* she was snatched up by Alfred Hitchcock to star in some of his best thrillers, including *Rear Window* with James Stewart. Hitchcock was convinced that none of the directors who had worked with her previously had caught the excitement of her 'ice and fire' personality. He talked of her latent 'wit and sexuality' which he was determined to bring out; became first obsessed with her, then infatuated.

There was no doubt she caused havoc in the hearts of many of her leading men. Ray Milland, for example, became so infatuated when they were making *Dial M for Murder* that he pretended that he had separated from his wife so that he could pursue her. There was a strong mutual attraction between her and William Holden but as he was already married to a charming wife

Grace rapidly stepped out of the situation. Most difficult of all was the passion she stirred up in the heart of Bing Crosby who, after first opposing the choice of Grace to play opposite him in *The Country Girl*, proceeded to fall desperately in love with her during filming.

By the spring of 1954 Grace Kelly's personal life was one of the favourite topics of Hollywood gossip. Who would be the one to melt the ice maiden? She deeply resented this intrusion into her privacy and the misrepresentation of so many of her friendships. Early in her career there had been a sad love affair with actor Gene Lyons, who had drink problems, and she had enjoyed a gay romance with handsome French film star Jean Pierre Aumont, but none of her emotional relationships had ended satisfactorily. Now in 1954 she was introduced to Oleg Cassini, couturier and cosmopolitan, who had once been married to actress Gene Tierney. Cassini was in a different league to most of the men Grace had been romantically connected with. Handsome, urbane, an old-fashioned courtier, he was the son of Countess Marguerite Cassini, daughter of Tsar Nicholas II's ambassador to the United States, and Alexander Loiewski of the Imperial Russian foreign service. Cassini set out to woo her in style, sending armfuls of roses to her apartment every day. But as a twice divorced man he was regarded as a non-starter by the Kelly family and with their implacable opposition to him it looked like another romantic shipwreck.

Fortunately this same year was proving to be a triumph for her career. She won an Oscar for her part in *The Country Girl* and was considered box-office magic by the Hollywood moguls. She had also been cast opposite Cary Grant in her third picture for Hitchcock, a witty, delightful romp called *To Catch a Thief* and it was to be filmed on location on the Riviera. Hitchcock called Edith Head, who was designing the costumes, and told her to make Grace Kelly look like a princess. The designer created a fantastic wardrobe. At the masked ball, which was the film's climax, Grace caused gasps of admiration when she appeared in a magnificent gold silk ball gown, her hair and skin glistening as if covered with gold leaf.

Grace Kelly loved the Riviera. To her it had always seemed the most beautiful place in Europe. But she had never been to Monaco and confessed she was longing to have a chance to play roulette at the casino in Monte Carlo. One day, during a break from filming, Betsy Drake, Cary Grant's wife, suggested they should get up a small party and spend the day there. Steven Englund, Grace Kelly's biographer, tells how Grace was taken for a drive round the Principality before going to the casino. She was enchanted by everything she saw and particularly intrigued by the description of some wonderful gardens on a high plateau called 'The Rock'.

'Whose gardens are those?' she asked.

'Prince Grimaldi's,' someone replied. 'I hear he's a stuffy fellow.'

'Oh, I'd like to see his flowers,' said Grace wistfully. She was to get her wish, but not until the following spring when she went to the palace with *Paris Match* and walked through the gardens with the man who owned them.

Prince Rainier, the thirty-two-year-old ruler of Monaco, descendant of an unbroken line of Grimaldis going back to the thirteenth century, was in fact quite the reverse of stuffy. Some thought him a little too daring. Like all the Grimaldis he had a passionate love of anything to do with the sea. Not only was he a skilled yachtsman but he was fascinated by underwater research and sometimes took part in skin-diving explorations. Mad about motor-racing – his idol was the Argentinian ace, Fangio – he sometimes took part in competitive races incognito. In 1953 he entered the Tour de France under an assumed name, crashed into a tree and nearly put an end to the Grimaldi dynasty. He was badly concussed and his advisers were relieved to find he was temporarily cured of his passion for racing-cars.

Rainier had not had a very happy childhood. His parents were estranged and he was left a great deal to his own devices, making him in many ways unsure of himself and slightly edgy with strangers. However, when he ascended the throne at the death of his grandfather, Louis II, on 9 May 1949, he surprised a great many people by the way in which he applied himself to his task. The Principality was nothing like the glamorous playground for the jet set that it has become today. Rainier realized he had to modernize it. Some of the more moribund members of his secretariat were replaced with younger and more forward-looking men. He gave orders for drastic reconstruction work such as driving a tunnel through The Rock and reclaiming more land from the sea. Plans were set in motion to attract tourists and the rich punters.

The Monagasques thought a great deal of their young Prince but by 1955 they were beginning to express the hope that he would soon find himself a Princess. They knew he had a close liaison with Gisèle Pascal, the glamorous French film actress, and that his feelings were deeply involved, but the relationship was frowned upon. For one thing it was said her parents ran a fruit and vegetable stall in the market at Nice and this did not fit in with Monaco's idea of a consort for a Grimaldi. People were relieved when his affair with Gisèle Pascal ended but noticed he still avoided his mother's match-making parties at the family's ancestral château at Marchais in France.

By the spring of 1955, when Grace Kelly went to the Cannes Film Festival and met Prince Rainier for the first time, he was regarded as one of the most eligible royals in Europe. The people of Monaco, however, had almost resigned themselves to having a bachelor Prince. He did not seem to have any interest in the beautiful young aristocrats, eminently suitable, who drifted in and out of the social season. Did they but know it, the wheels of fate had started to turn. That summer Rainier found himself deeply involved in a serious financial crisis but his American chaplain, friend and confidant, Father Tucker, knew that Grace Kelly was also on his mind.

Before the season ended Russell Austin, a wealthy oilman from New Jersey and a close friend of the Kelly family, arrived from the U.S. with his wife, Edith, to spend a few weeks on the Riviera. Learning that the Sports Club of Monaco was holding its first gala of the season, they applied for tickets, only to be told that all the tables had been booked weeks ago. Half jokingly Edith suggested they ought to contact Prince Rainier, tell him they were old friends of Grace Kelly and ask if he could help them get a table. Russell was reluctant at first but eventually, reckoning he had nothing to lose, called the palace and left a message with one of the Prince's secretaries. The Austins got their tickets. Even better, they received a phone call from Father Tucker who said His Serene Highness would be delighted to meet any friend of Miss Kelly and would they join him for tea next day?

Russell Austin said afterwards that Rainier had talked of 'nothing but Grace' and seemed interested in anything he had to say

35

about the Kelly family. The meeting was formal but the good-natured American invited his host to visit him any time he was in the U.S.A. Rainier assured him he would take advantage of the offer should the opportunity arise.

The Prince had faced some difficult financial problems that year and needed a break. When Father Tucker told him he had to return to America in December to renew his vows at his home church, Rainier decided he would go too. He had long promised himself a trip to the States. The palace in Monaco issued a statement saying that His Serene Highness was going on a strictly private visit. He would have a routine medical check-up at the Johns Hopkins Hospital in New York then travel south to fish for barracuda off the Florida coast.

Under the name of 'Mr Grimaldi' he sailed from Le Havre on 8 December, Father Tucker having already been in touch with the Austins, who had invited Rainier to spend Christmas Eve with them at their home in Margate, New Jersey. On his arrival the Austins passed on another invitation from the Kelly family asking him to spend Christmas with them at their mansion in East Falls, Philadelphia.

Grace knew that Prince Rainier was in America. She had been on location in North Carolina filming *The Swan* with Alec Guinness when one of his secretaries phoned to say the Prince would like to visit Miss Kelly on the set and watch the film being made. Did she mind? Grace said she would not mind in the least but when a reporter from *Look* magazine asked her the question that everyone wanted to ask she said icily, 'If you think there's some romance going on, you're wrong. I haven't heard one word from him.'

He did not manage to get to North Carolina before the film crew packed up for the holiday. Instead, Grace arrived home to be told by her excited mother that Prince Rainier would be spending Christmas with them.

The very fact that the Prince was away from home at such a time seemed significant to many people in Monaco. They knew that the dressing of the Christmas tree at the palace was a tradition very dear to his heart and one that he would not lightly miss. However, when his Christmas message was transmitted from America to the people of Monaco there was no hint of anything special. If he was staying in America over Christmas for something of importance, he gave no indication of what it was in his broadcast.

Christmas dinner at the Kelly mansion was a splendid affair which the presence of a real, live Prince made even more magical. Grace, nervous but excited at the prospect of seeing Rainier again, looked more beautiful than ever in the light of the Christmas candles. While everyone enjoyed themselves in high party spirits, they danced together all evening, then drifted off, deep in conversation. Rainier had only intended to stay for a few hours but ended by staying the night.

They spent several days together in Philadelphia before Grace returned to her apartment in New York. Rainier postponed his return to Monaco and followed her, obviously determined not to let her out of his sight. Five days after she had met him for the second time, Grace called her mother to tell her she was 'very much in love'. Prince Rainier had confessed in more or less the same words to Father Tucker.

According to Steven Englund, Father Tucker and Grace's parents met for dinner on 30 December at the Austins' house in New Jersey. The priest informed the Kellys that Rainier wished to marry their daughter. Margaret Kelly could hardly contain her joy but Jack only gave his consent after being assured that the Prince was indeed 'noble not only by birth but by deed and character'.

There was a celebration lunch in Philadelphia next day at which Grace Kelly was seen to be wearing a magnificent twelve-carat solitaire diamond ring. She was radiant. Rainier, too, by every gesture gave himself away as a man deeply in love. What made him especially happy was the fact that he could see Grace had all the qualities to make a princess. Added to this was the blessed fact that she was a devout Catholic who had declared that when she married it would be for ever. There could not have been any question of Rainier marrying a non-Catholic. The Grimaldis are Catholic princes closely associated with the Vatican, a fact which perhaps impressed the Kellys more than anything.

On the evening of 4 January, when their engagement was still only family knowledge, Grace and Rainier were seen together at the Stork Club in New York. As they left, they were surrounded by reporters. Was there a romance? Were they in love? Grace replied with a huge smile, 'Nothing to say,' adding mischievously, 'Yet.' Both knew their precious days of privacy were coming to an end. The following day their engagement was announced officially and the press went wild with stories about their 'lightning romance'. Rainier telephoned Monaco and authorized his Minister of State to break the news. Grace telephoned her friends. They confessed they were staggered by the news. She had never even mentioned his name. Was it a marriage of state? Nobody seeing the two of them together could imagine for a second that it was an arranged affair. As Prince Rainier said years later, 'We just fell in love very quickly.' It was significant that when Grace Kelly came to tell her friends of her engagement she blurted out, 'I'm in love with a wonderful man.' The fact that he was the Prince of Monaco came second.

Once the news had been released, both of them were besieged by reporters and photographers, who knew they had the romantic story of the decade on their hands. Sometimes Rainier lost his patience with the never-ending and often impertinent questions put to him by American newspapermen. Not used to royalty, they called him 'imperious'. But even Grace Kelly began to feel the strain and was glad when in the middle of January she had to return to work.

She had been cast as Tracy Lord in *High Society*, a plum part that Katharine Hepburn played in an earlier version, and it was proving to be her favourite film. She came across on the screen as more beautiful and seductive than ever before, delighted to be working with Bing Crosby and Frank Sinatra and conscious of the fact that this could be her last film. She still had four years of her contract to run and Hollywood was full of speculation as to whether she would continue to film after she became Princess Grace. Rainier immediately put a stop to that at one of his short-tempered meetings with the press. Marriage, he informed everyone, would, of course, mean the end of her acting career. How could it be otherwise?

Prince Rainier had spent a month in Hollywood with Grace while she was filming, but by the middle of February he decided it was time for him to return to Monaco. He tried to get out of the country incognito but to no avail. He was pursued to the bitter end until someone asked him if he was not weary of the publicity. 'A little bit,' he sighed, 'but I expect people will soon get sick of all these stories.' On the contrary, people were avid for every detail about this romantic couple.

The wedding was fixed for 18 April and it was announced that it would take place at the Cathedral of St Nicholas in Monaco where all previous Grimaldi princes had been married. For one moment Grace Kelly's parents had imagined her getting married from home like other people's daughters and they were ready to spend a fortune to provide Philadelphia with a royal occasion. But Rainier explained he had been in touch with his government and there was no question of the wedding being held anywhere but in Monaco. That, he explained gently, was how it had to be when a girl married the ruler of another country. The Principality, thrilled to the core, started to prepare.

Once the filming of *High Society* was finished, Grace gave herself up to an endless round of parties, celebrations and farewells. The last two weeks in New York were spent shopping for her trousseau. Her studio, M.G.M., had already given her all the beautiful clothes she wore in *High Society* to start her off. The most expensive thing she bought apart from some fabulous ball gowns was a full-length Canadian sable coat. Her style was elegant, uncluttered, and girls all over the world were already trying to copy it, to their advantage. As though to ensure that she took something of her old life with her she crammed half a dozen pairs of worn jeans and shirts into the suitcases on top of her finery.

New York gave her a ticker-tape farewell when she sailed on the liner *Constitution* with a sizable party made up of the Kelly family and friends. Monaco was in a state of ferment. It was estimated that 1,800 reporters and photographers were milling around the Principality, leaving hardly a square inch to stand on. It was learned that the *Constitution*, due on 12 April, would have to dock at Cannes first to unload Miss Kelly's luggage. It amounted to two lorry loads. But a spectacular welcome had been planned for her.

Prince Rainier intended to sail out to meet the liner and take his bride on to his yacht *Deo Juvante II*, all decked out in the Grimaldi colours. Unfortunately, rain and strong winds forecast the evening before had produced a heavy swell. For half an hour the yacht tried to come alongside the liner without much success. The two vessels dipped and rolled in a sickening fashion. At last there came a moment of calm and Grace was able to walk down the gangplank carpeted with red carnations while thousands

39

more flowers thrown by passengers on the *Constitution* fluttered around her and floated on the sea. On board his yacht Prince Rainier greeted her quite formally, taking both her hands in his. There was no kiss or embrace for the public eye.

Along the quaysides crowds had been waiting for hours to catch a glimpse of the film star who was soon to become a princess. As the *Deo Juvante* sailed into harbour the sun broke through the clouds and the air exploded with sound as hundreds of ships' sirens hooted their welcome and a twenty-one-gun salute boomed out from the shore. A mammoth firework display went up from the Onassis yacht spreading the Grimaldi blazon across the sky. Slowly the *Deo Juvante* made her way through a flotilla of beflagged boats until she came to her mooring.

It was noon when Grace, clutching her pet poodle, stepped ashore and waved to the crowds. They went wild. She was wearing a simple navy-blue silk dress to which was pinned a spray of pale mauve orchids. A large-brimmed white organdie hat partly concealed the emotion on her face from the cameras. Once they were inside the palace, however, the intensity of the experience proved too much. She broke down and wept on Rainier's shoulder. He tenderly put his arms around her, brushed away her tears, spoke softly for her alone. The room cleared and the couple were left together for a brief spell. It did not take her long to recover. She had soon powdered her nose and smoothed her hair and appeared on Rainier's arm looking cool and radiant. 'It's just one of the penalties of being a princess,' he teased her.

As wedding stories streamed across the world's front pages, wedding presents streamed into the palace. Prince Rainier's subjects had given him a Rolls-Royce; Aristotle Onassis, the Greek shipping millionaire whose yacht *Christina* was anchored in Monaco harbour, presented Grace with an exquisite ruby bracelet and the croupiers at Monte Carlo casino sent a hand-carved ivory chess set.

The seven days leading up to the wedding were bedlam, with reporters and photographers outnumbering the Monagasque army eight to one. There was hardly a spare inch of Monaco to stand on. Neither Grace nor Rainier had really anticipated the intense interest their wedding would cause and they began to wish they could sneak away and be married by a village priest at a little chapel in the mountains.

On the morning of 18 April a civil marriage ceremony took place in the throne room at the palace. Prince Rainier wore a formal black morning suit and Grace was dressed in rose-coloured Alençon lace. Both seemed to be slightly nervous and answered 'Oui' to each question in barely audible voices. A full nuptial mass at the Cathedral was to be held next day.

At 10.35 a.m., her face half hidden by a tulle veil, Grace walked up the nave of the Cathedral on her father's arm. Her ivory-coloured dress with its close bodice of old-rose point Brussels lace, its skirt billowing out in yards and yards of rustling silk and taffeta, emphasized the classic quality of her beauty. Her blonde, silky hair was drawn back into a chignon and held by a tiny medieval headdress of lace and pearls. Prince Rainier, in full-dress uniform with a sash of the red and white Grimaldi colours, could hardly take his eyes off her.

Six hundred guests crammed into the Cathedral. There was a large contingent of Kellys, and Hollywood was represented by Cary Grant, David Niven and Ava Gardner. The atmosphere was heavy with the smell of white lilac, which smothered the high altar and hung in great golden baskets from the ceiling.

For Grace, deeply religious, it was, as she said afterwards one of the most tremendous moments of her life. Throughout, she seemed unaware of anyone else but the man who was to become her husband and the bishop who heard their vows. Those vows had to be taken under a merciless battery of lights, with TV cameras ready to record every tiny movement.

Prince Rainier took a gold ring from a white satin cushion and placed it on her finger. The tension was broken for a moment as Grace tried to push a ring on to his finger, and it stuck. For a few seconds they struggled together to get it on. Once the ring was in place they gazed at each other and her eyes filled with tears. At that moment it was certain no one else existed for them.

Rainier and his princess emerged arm-in-arm from the Cathedral into brilliant sunshine to be greeted by ecstatic crowds. After the reception, at which more people seemed to be crowded into the palace than would have been thought possible, the couple sailed off in the *Deo Juvante* accompanied by the screeching of sirens. Longing to be alone, their honeymoon cruise took them to Majorca and around the Spanish coast.

Years later, when she was being interviewed for a magazine

Princess Grace told the interviewer, 'When I married Prince Rainier I married the man, not what he was or who he was. I fell in love with him, no matter how it might all turn out.' It turned out well. Grace Kelly, it seemed, had all the qualities needed for a modern princess. Her Serene Highness, underneath the high-gloss, delicate exterior, was a committed, thoughtful woman who backed her husband to the hilt.

From the start they worked together. She set about modernizing the palace by suggesting they install lifts and central heating. 'It was a bit mothballish before she came,' Rainier admitted. She supervised the redecoration of rooms so that they became light and airy and planned the layout of a beautiful new tropical garden round the swimming pool. In other words, she made a comfortable, attractive home for Rainier out of the gloomy labyrinth of the old palace.

As the years went by the Prince came to admire not only her feminine qualities as a wife and mother but her business acumen and her shrewd observance of international personalities, diplomats and politicians. She had set out immediately to improve her schoolgirl French until she was fluent, and did her homework on European politics. She charmed everyone, even General de Gaulle, who listened to her with the sort of attention he rarely gave to anyone.

But her greatest energies were given to anything to do with children, whether they were sick, deprived, clever or talented. While Rainier gave his attention to government, she spread her patronage and help over as many charities as possible. But because he loved and respected her, Rainier discussed everything with Princess Grace and preferred that they worked as a team on anything to do with Monaco.

Their eldest daughter, Caroline, was born to the sound of a twenty-one-gun salute on 23 January 1957. Fifteen months later Princess Grace gave birth to a son, Albert, who became heir to the throne. Their youngest daughter, Stephanie, was not born until 1965.

Princess Grace came to be regarded as a model wife and mother by the Catholic Church but her influence was in fact much wider. She liked to think of herself as a modern, contemporary woman capable of dealing with all the different problems that arise both inside and outside the home. She came to hate her image as a fairy-tale princess because it made people think of her as someone set apart in a gilded cage. She began to interest herself more and more in the problems of her adopted country. The Principality had been in dire financial trouble before she married Prince Rainier. The Greek shipping magnate Aristotle Onassis had bought a controlling interest in its greatest asset, the Casino in Monte Carlo, and, many suspected, had ambitions to take over much more. Rainier had fortunately managed to regain control of the Casino's 'bank'. To the surprise of many, the lovely Princess Grace not only demonstrated that she understood high finance but also that she had the grasp of a clear-thinking business woman.

She wanted Monaco to mean much more to the world than just a sunspot for jet-setting millionaires and gamblers. As the Casino was the one internationally known feature of Monaco she set out to enhance its image. It would be a good idea, she suggested, if major cultural and social events were held there rather than at the palace. The idea was adopted and the lavishness and glamour of her international charity balls and ballet performances drew the rich and famous from all over the world. Prince Rainier delighted in her efforts.

With the passage of years the Grimaldis became one of the most glamorous and attractive royal families in Europe. Princess Grace kept her remarkable beauty, eventually becoming a little fuller in the figure but always appearing in public superbly dressed. Prince Rainier, now distinguished with grey-white hair, always looked proud of his family. Of their children Caroline and Stephanie were to give their parents monumental headaches with their temperamental behaviour and unsuitable love affairs, but Prince Albert, the apple of his mother's eye, took his role as heir to the throne with shy, unassuming sincerity.

The romance did not end with their marriage. That was obvious every time they allowed cameras into the palace to film their private lives. For years Grace and Rainier loved to dance cheek to cheek after dinner to American records sent over by Mrs Kelly. At weekends and in the hot summer months they loved to escape to their ranch house up in the mountains at Roc Agel. Here the Prince had a hut for his carpentry and metalwork. He drove a tractor and worked on his tiny dairy farm and in his orchard. Princess Grace, her hair tied up in a scarf, would take over the kitchen and cook excellent curries, Chinese dishes and the Polynesian food her husband loved.

As Monaco flourished and became not only a tourist paradise but the favourite playground for the rich and beautiful, the demands on both of them became greater. They never seemed to have enough time together. Grace wanted more than anything to have a year alone with her husband.

In the summer of 1982 they had managed to slip away for a wonderful cruise by themselves to Norway. But the autumn ahead was packed with charity balls and galas and their daughter Stephanie was in the midst of an emotional trauma. They had to get her to buckle down to her studies. Then there was a trip to the States to be planned.

Strangely enough, in the light of what happened, it was Princess Grace who always worried about Rainier when it came to driving. He still had some of the old racing blood in him once he got behind the wheel of a car and she continually urged him not to take corners too fast. Grace was not a natural driver and preferred to be chauffeur driven, though she did take the wheel when necessary.

It seemed to be necessary on the morning of Monday, 13 September. The royal family had spent the weekend at Roc Agel. Grace planned to take Stephanie back to the palace but as she had laid out several evening dresses on the back seat of her Rover 3500 there was no room for three people. The chauffeur would have to stay behind.

Princess Grace and Stephanie left Roc Agel at around 9.30 a.m. She took the winding mountain road very slowly. Her children always joked that if they set off on foot they would probably reach the palace before her. All the sharp hair-pin bends were protected with barriers to stop careless drivers shooting off and down the sheer drop of the mountain side – all but one, the last. Princess Grace had negotiated all the worst bends and was within sight of the palace and the final curve in the road when it happened. She could not have been driving faster than twenty-five to thirty miles an hour when a lorry driver following the Rover saw it suddenly begin to zig-zag, then career right off the road and down the mountain side. When rescuers reached them, Princess Grace was completely unconscious and Stephanie was lying in a state of shock, having apparently tried to reach across her mother and gain control of the car.

What really happened no one was ever quite sure but it was thought that Princess Grace probably had a slight stroke while at the wheel of the car and that her daughter had tried to save them both. But nothing could save Princess Grace. In a matter of hours she had gone into a coma. On 14 September, at 9.30 in the morning, the life-support machine was disconnected.

One had only to glimpse the grief-stricken Rainier, white hair awry, tears streaming down his face, oblivious of everybody as he followed her coffin, to realize this had been a marriage of deep and lasting love. 'The years of Grace', as they began to be called, were over. But her memory is still fresh in the tiny country which made a film star into a princess.

# The Prince of Wales
## —AND—
# Lady Diana Spencer

**W**hen Prince Charles first saw Lady Diana Spencer she was sitting in a pram at Sandringham and he took about as much notice of her as the usual fourteen-year-old schoolboy takes of babies.

The Spencer family lived at Park House on the Sandringham estate only a few hundred yards from the royal family's Norfolk home. In her infant years, bouncy little Diana was a regular guest at parties for the younger royals, Princes Andrew and Edward, but saw little of their elder brother. When she was sent off to board at Riddlesworth Hall, a preparatory school near Diss in Norfolk, it was to Prince Andrew that Diana wrote her letters in a careful, schoolgirlish hand.

She was tall and gawky in her early teens. Prince Charles sometimes teased her but took out her elder sister, Sarah, a striking red-head who went skiing with him to Klosters in Switzerland and was named as a possible future bride. When he was invited to Sarah's ancestral home, Althorp in Northampton-shire, sixteen-year-old Diana was there, leggy and windblown, stomping about a ploughed field in Wellington boots. She looked, he thought, as though she could be good fun.

She had always been there, always in the background, the one who was invited 'for Andrew', the girl-next-door *par excellence*. But it wasn't until she was nineteen in the summer of 1980 that he turned and looked at her as if for the first time. To his amazement, the gangling, windswept girl had turned into a long-legged beauty with deep-blue eyes, thick honey-coloured hair and a most enticing, wistful smile. She was fun but she was also kind, adored children and knew her way in the royal world.

Without warning, the thirty-two-year-old bachelor prince was in love. He suddenly realized that she was the right girl to be his future queen. He had simply been waiting for her to grow up.

For several years Prince Charles had been urged by all those around him to find a bride. He was heir to the throne and he must have a wife. In a rash moment he had once declared that he thought 'a chap like me' ought to be settled by his thirtieth birthday, but it had come and gone without any announcement from the Palace. 'You'd better get on with it, Charles,' said his father, the Duke of Edinburgh, 'or there won't be anyone left.'

At thirty-two he was an extremely attractive man. His physique had been hardened by years of sport and tough discipline; his features, though far from classical, had taken on a quizzical appeal and were flattered by a longer hair style. He was bronzed, fit, and women began to throw themselves at him with obvious intent. He had had plenty of attractive and suitably aristo-cratic girlfriends and each one came in for fierce scrutiny as a 'possible'. But one by one they were allowed to drift off. Some married other suitably aristocratic young men, others were quietly dumped because of some episode or other in their past lives. Speculation reached fever pitch when it was rumoured that the Queen favoured Princess Marie-Astrid of Luxembourg, if only the problem of her Catholic religion could be overcome. But Charles was not to be hurried. His own parents, Queen Elizabeth and Prince Philip, Duke of Edinburgh, had married for love and he was determined to do the same.

For a royal prince, his upbringing had been enlightened and modern. Born on Sunday, 14 November 1948, his arrival brought rejoicing to a nation in the dreary aftermath of war. Beacons were lit from Land's End to John o'Groats and the fountains in Trafalgar Square were turned blue for a week. He was a lovable small boy. His grandfather, George VI, called him 'a sweet little chap' and his great-grandmother, Queen Mary, much mellowed by the years, allowed him to play with precious pieces of jade from her collection. He was barely three years old when George VI died, his mother became Queen and he was suddenly Duke of Cornwall and heir apparent.

Prince Philip was determined not to let him be dominated by nannies. He taught him to swim by the age of six, took him sailing in pretty rough weather and helped him overcome his fear of ponies so that he could ride. Charles became the first heir to the throne to go to school with other children, starting at a pre-preparatory school in Hans Place, Knightsbridge in London, then going on to Cheam at Headley on the Berkshire Downs. He was very miserable at first because he hated being away from home and the other pupils, not knowing quite how to treat him, left him alone. When he left four years later, however, it was with a good all-round report (apart from maths) and a footnote that he was 'considerate to others, open hearted and incapable of malice'.

On the advice of his father he was sent next to Prince Philip's old school, Gordonstoun in Scotland, a tough establishment run on spartan lines with the emphasis on creating a healthy body, self-reliance and self-confidence. The heir to the throne shared a bleak dormitory with bare wooden floorboards, unpainted walls and bare lightbulbs, washed in cold water and was submitted to a rigorous routine. Before his final year, when he was head boy, he was sent to Australia to spend a term at Geelong Grammar School, which was run very much on the lines of Gordonstoun. He found himself chopping wood and cleaning out pigsties at 'Timbertop', an outpost of Geelong on the slopes of the Great Dividing Range. But he loved every minute of it. He liked the Australians and they liked him. 'They got rid of my shyness,' he admitted afterwards. His education was completed at Trinity College, Cambridge, where he lived in rooms identical to those of other students, ate in the company of 230 other undergraduates and cycled to and from lectures wearing a tweed jacket and baggy flannels.

In spite of the toughening up process he still looked a very vulnerable young man when he was crowned Prince of Wales at a stunning ceremony at Caernarvon Castle in the summer of 1969. Fears were voiced that he might be in danger from the more active Welsh nationalists. But Charles had done his homework. He had spent two terms at the University College of Wales in Aberystwyth and he had taken the trouble to learn the Welsh language. His interest in Wales was genuine and sincere and he was accepted with warmth and affection.

After he left university and entered fully into royal life his good-natured personality, revealed in a series of broadcasts and TV appearances, made him a very popular figure. He identified himself with the young, founded a series of trusts for youth, began to travel abroad and proved a splendid ambassador for British industry. But it was not until he finished his six-year stint with the Services that he really emerged in his late twenties as a full-blown personality, attractive to the opposite sex.

After serving on a coastal minesweeper, then as a navigation officer in the Caribbean, he was awarded his pilot's wings, learned to fly a helicopter and trained as a commando. Socially he was a polo-playing bachelor who had no difficulty at all in finding pretty companions.

One of his earliest girlfriends was Lucia Santa Cruz, daughter of the Chilean ambassador. They met at Cambridge when she was research assistant to Lord Butler, the Master of Trinity College, and she was his guest at the party which followed his Investiture at Caernarvon. When she disappeared, Georgina Russell, attractive blonde daughter of Britain's ambassador in Brazil, was often seen with him at polo matches, and for a time he escorted Lady Leonora Grosvenor, daughter of the Duke of Westminster, who was later to marry Patrick, Earl of Lichfield. Highly favoured as a possible bride was Lady Jane Wellesley, daughter of the Duke of Wellington, who lasted for four years, off and on, stayed at Sandringham and invited Charles to spend a holiday on her family's estate in Spain. But in 1974 she gave a dinner party and introduced him to Davina Sheffield, a pretty blonde, related to the Duke of Beaufort, who became his constant companion for two years. She had lots of character and at the height of the Vietnamese war went out to Saigon to work in an orphanage. The romance came to a sudden end when one of her former boyfriends told the press they had once spent several months in a cottage near Winchester.

Towards the end of 1976, while Charles was happily escorting one young socialite after another, there were endless press stories about a possible marriage with the Catholic Princess Marie-Astrid of Luxembourg. Charles eventually issued a hot denial through the Palace, pointing out that he did not even know the lady 'and people who do not know each other do not get engaged'. By June 1977 he was escorting the elegant Lady Camilla Fane, daughter of the Earl of Westmorland, and appeared with her at Ascot; he took the Duke of Rutland's daughter, Lady Charlotte Manners, to parties and theatres and was seen with

Mick Jagger's ex-girlfriend, Sabrina Guinness. His most constant companion at this time, however, was Diana's elder sister, Lady Sarah Spencer.

In November 1977, after a day's shooting there was a candlelit dinner at the Spencers' home. Lady Sarah made a grand entrance on the arm of the Prince of Wales. Diana watched with huge eyes. It was the first formal, grown-up dinner she had been allowed to attend and the guest of honour seemed to her an immensely attractive figure.

Though they were, and are, good friends, there was nothing serious in the relationship between Prince Charles and Lady Sarah. 'Charles is a fabulous person – but I'm not in love with him,' she told everyone after a skiing holiday in 1978. She went off and married someone else. Charles celebrated his thirtieth birthday with a party for nearly three hundred guests and left the world guessing as far as romance was concerned. He was still looking for that very special girl.

Lady Diana Spencer was born on the Queen's estate at Sandringham, Norfolk on 1 July 1961 at Park House, a solid country residence rented from the royal family. She was the third daughter of Edward Spencer, Viscount Althorp, heir to the seventh Earl Spencer, and his wife Frances, younger daughter of the fourth Baron Fermoy. Diana's father, 'Johnny' Spencer as he was always known, had been an equerry to King George VI and later to Queen Elizabeth II. He accompanied her on her Coronation tour of Australia in 1954. Diana's grandmother Ruth, Lady Fermoy, was Woman of the Bedchamber to the Queen Mother and one of her oldest friends. All four of her grandparents had served the Crown in one way or another. In other words, both sides of her family were steeped in the tradition of service to the royal family and had illustrious ancestors of their own going back to Saxon times.

Mixing with young royals from time to time was taken as a natural part of her life. Her upbringing was quite strict, but full of special treats. On her seventh birthday, for instance, her father hired a camel called Bert to give all the children rides. He felt very responsible for his children's happiness. The Althorp marriage was not successful. Diana was only six when her mother left home, eight when her parents were divorced in a highly publicized case in which Viscount Althorp sued his wife

51

for adultery with Peter Shand Kydd. Diana nevertheless remained close to her mother and frequently spent time with her on the island of Seil off north-west Scotland where Shand Kydd had an extensive sheep farm.

At the age of ten, with a trunk labelled 'D. Spencer', she was sent off to boarding school. Two years later, in 1973, she moved to West Heath, an exlusive girls' school near Sevenoaks, Kent, where she shared a dormitory with six other girls. They all had a bit of a crush on Prince Charles and pinned up on the wall a huge picture of him in full regalia. She was very popular, a cheerful, outgoing girl, always ready to help but not over ambitious as far as things like 'A' levels were concerned. On her mother's advice she was sent to complete her education at a finishing school at Chateau d'Oex, near Gstaad in Switzerland, where she took classes in domestic science, dressmaking, cooking and typing. She only stayed for one term.

By this time her father had succeeded to the family title and as the eighth Earl Spencer moved with his family into the stately Althorp set in 1,500 acres of beautiful Northamptonshire parkland. He had also married for the second time, his new wife being the former Countess of Dartmouth, a glamorous and dynamic figure much known for her public activities and for the fact that she was the daughter of romantic novelist Barbara Cartland. At first the Spencer children regarded her with trepidation but when, with great devotion, she nursed Lord Spencer through a crippling stroke in 1978, their attitude towards her changed considerably.

After leaving her finishing school Diana returned to London to live for a time at her mother's flat in Cadogan Square. She had already discovered that she liked being with small children and had a special rapport with them. For a year or so she offered her services to married friends as an unpaid nanny and children's help but in the spring of 1979, being totally disinterested in the ritual of 'coming out', she found a regular job at a nursery school, the Young England Kindergarten in Pimlico. Seeing that she intended to lead an independent life, Lord Spencer bought her a three-bedroomed flat in Coleherne Court, a mansion block off Old Brompton Road. She had great fun decorating it in modern pastel colours, then invited three friends, one of them, Carolyn Pride, an old chum from West Heath, to join her. Her life centred on her work at the Pimlico nursery school but in off-duty hours she led an active social life, thoroughly enjoying simple treats like a visit to the local cinema or meeting a few friends for drinks at a local pub. There were plenty of invitations to dinners, parties, theatres and weekends in the country when she would either take friends home to Althorp or visit other splendid houses belonging to people in her circle.

Sometimes she was invited to join the royal party either at Sandringham or Balmoral along with other young people of Prince Andrew's age. Prince Charles, though surrounded by his own friends, began to gaze more and more in the direction of this lovely young girl he had known since she was in her pram. Besides having blossomed into a beauty she had such good humour and charm she seemed to brighten up every room she walked into. She was obviously a great favourite with the Queen and the Queen Mother.

Probably it was in February 1980, when she was invited to join the royal party at Sandringham and travelled to Norfolk with Amanda Knatchbull, grand-daughter of Earl Mountbatten, that the love story of Prince Charles and Lady Diana really began and he saw her as the girl he had been looking for all those years.

That summer three events occurred that brought them together in a new way. In July Prince Charles asked her if she would like to watch a polo match at Cowdray Park, near Midhurst in Sussex. The Prince was playing for Les Diables Bleus and Diana, with the rest of the party, watched from Lord Cowdray's stand in the members' enclosure. Not a particularly 'horsey' girl, her interest was obviously more on the suntanned, athletic prince than on the game he was playing. During August and Cowes Week on the Isle of Wight a radiant, nineteen-year-old Diana was principal guest of the Prince of Wales on board the Royal Yacht *Britannia*. They were seen laughing and chatting together and at one point she ducked her royal host in the Solent by flipping the mast of his windsurfer – but still nothing was thought of it as Prince Andrew, Prince Edward and their cousins James and Marina Ogilvy were also in the party. Early in September she was a royal guest again, this time at Balmoral. By now columnist Nigel Dempster had rumbled that something was in the air and asked in the *Daily Mail*, 'Has Charles found his future bride?' Photographers flocked to Scotland armed with long-range cameras. One telephoto lens aimed at Charles salmon fishing in the River Dee also picked up Lady Diana Spencer in charge of a picnic basket on the bank. From then on it was open season for the press.

Throughout the summer of 1980 Diana had told friends that she was going out with a Charles Renfrew. Before they could tumble to the fact that Baron Renfrew was one of the Prince of Wales' titles the whole thing was out in the open.

For the next five months Diana came under relentless pressure from an ever attendant press. From dawn to dusk she was followed, photographed and questioned. Eventually the pressure became so great that her mother Mrs Shand Kydd wrote to *The Times* protesting at what almost amounted to the persecution of her daughter. Charles greatly feared that her ordeal at the hands of the media would frighten her off and cause her to sever their relationship. But she coped admirably, responding with a shy smile and flushed cheeks, once blurting out, 'You know I can't say anything about the Prince or my feelings for him.' Charles and the rest of the royal family watched her performance with growing admiration.

They met in secret and at friends' houses but on 4 November, when six of Princess Margaret's friends gave a dance for her at the Ritz Hotel in London to celebate her fiftieth birthday, Diana was among the two hundred guests and at the dinner beforehand sat next to the Prince of Wales. Rumour spread that the Prince would announce their engagement on his thirty-second birthday on 14 November but the day came and went without a word from the Palace, and the Prince flew off to make an official tour of India and Nepal, which included a three-day trek in the Himalayas. In India it was pointedly brought to his notice that there was a legend which said that any man who visited the Taj Mahal as a bachelor would one day return with a wife.

By now it was obvious to all those close to them that the couple were in love but Charles, perhaps fearful of rejection by this delightful but strong-willed girl thirteen years younger than himself, could not bring himself to propose. It is said that at one stage of their courtship Charles tried to find out Diana's views on marriage in a roundabout fashion as they walked together in a friend's garden. 'If someone were to ask you ... what would you think?' His look of anxiety and the obvious reason for the question were said to have tickled her sense of humour and her reply was accompanied by stifled giggles.

That Christmas the Prince spent the holiday with his family at Windsor and Diana travelled north to Althorp. There were glimpses of her at Sandringham over the New Year but Charles went alone for a skiing holiday to Klosters and there was no sign of Diana on the slopes. Things looked ominously uncertain when it was learned that Diana was flying out to Australia with her mother and step-father to spend a holiday with them on their sheep farm in New South Wales.

The day before her departure on 6 February the Prince went out on manoeuvres in the Channel on H.M.S. *Invincible*, the Navy's latest aircraft carrier. He returned to London that evening and dined with Diana in his apartment at Buckingham Palace. It was then that he proposed. The Prince, still diffident, told her she need not give her answer immediately. She could, he suggested, think it over while she was in Australia. But Diana had no doubts. She accepted at once.

Before leaving she told her flatmates and they opened a bottle of champagne. Her departure on a scheduled QANTAS flight was by some miracle kept secret. She travelled out with her mother and step-father, excited at this, her first visit to Australia, and managed to arrive undetected at the Shand Kydd sheep station at Yass. Before long, however, the Australian press descended by helicopter and the family had to seek refuge with a friend at a beach house on the coast of New South Wales.

Back in London towards the end of February Diana kept a low profile, though she managed to see Prince Charles at Highgrove, his home near Tetbury in Gloucestershire, and was with him when his favourite horse Allibar had a heart attack and died. A few days after this incident, which upset them both, Prince Charles telephoned Althorp and asked Earl Spencer for his daughter's hand in marriage. Consent was readily given.

At last, on Tuesday, 24 February at 11 a.m. months of speculation came to an end with an announcement from Buckingham Palace:

It is with the greatest pleasure that the Queen and the Duke of Edinburgh announce the betrothal of their beloved son, the Prince of Wales, to the Lady Diana Spencer, daughter of the Earl Spencer and the Honourable Mrs Shand Kydd.

Though it was still midwinter the news seemed to bring a touch of spring to Britain where people openly expressed their delight that Prince Charles had chosen such a thoroughly English rose to be his bride. When they appeared before the cameras she blushed prettily and lowered her eyelashes but proved that she had a quick and ready wit by parrying awkward questions as fast as they were put to her. On the third finger of her left hand sparkled an enormous sapphire surrounded by diamonds.

Life changed overnight for the future Princess of Wales. Almost immediately she had to say goodbye to her life at the Pimlico kindergarten and leave the flat which she had shared with her three girlfriends for the past two years. From then until the wedding she was provided with a suite of rooms in Buckingham Palace and given a private secretary to answer the thousands upon thousands of congratulatory letters and telegrams arriving from all over the world.

On 3 March they appeared together in public for the first time since their engagement, paying a private visit to the opera to see Meyerbeer's *L'Africaine*. The excitement they created was nothing compared to their first official appearance six days later at a reception at the Goldsmiths' Hall in the City of London. On this occasion Diana appeared in a low-cut, strapless black silk taffeta ballgown which created a sensation. She looked stunning and not at all demure, and the Prince of Wales looked justly proud of her. The dress had been designed by David and Elizabeth Emanuel and soon it was learned that they had also been chosen to design the wedding dress. This was an obvious break with tradition and indicated that Diana would be setting her own trends in fashion.

The wedding itself, planned for 29 July, was obviously going to be a brilliant occasion for which all the splendour of State, all the colour and tradition of royal celebration would provide a feast for the eyes of the world. Prince Charles had chosen St Paul's Cathedral for the ceremony rather than Westminster Abbey. For one thing, he pointed out, it held more people. He also admitted that he liked the ambience of St Paul's and frequently popped in there for a private visit.

As dawn broke on the great day London was bathed in a warm golden haze. The night before a crowd of half a million people, happy and enthusiastic, packed into Hyde Park to watch two and a half tons of fireworks blaze up into the London sky. They also watched Prince Charles light the first of a chain of beacons that stretched from end to end of the country in a ring of fire. Royal observer Robert Lacey wrote of the relaxed, happy, patriotic crowds, 'People seemed to feel that the marriage of this young couple was somehow hopeful, positive, regenerating....'

Diana, who was to leave for her wedding from the Queen Mother's London home, Clarence House, was awakened at 6 a.m. and it was not long before Kevin Stanley, her hairdresser from the flat-sharing days, arrived to arrange her hair. He was followed by make-up artist Barbara Daley, who concentrated on giving the bride a natural look, then by couturiers David and Elizabeth Emanuel, anxious to see that their bridal gown was carefully unpacked from its sea of tissue paper.

As she drove out through the gates of Clarence House in the Glass Coach with her father by her side, those who had vantage points craned their necks to see her, but it was not until she started to walk up the steps of St Paul's that the full splendour of the royal bride could be seen. She was a wonderfully romantic figure in a dress of ivory silk taffeta and old lace embroidered with sequins and pearls, the huge, thistledown crinoline skirt billowing around her, its train seeming to go on for ever. The Spencer tiara held her full veil in place and she remained veiled for the first part of the ceremony. Earl Spencer, the proudest man in England, still suffering some difficulties in walking as a result of his stroke, clasped his daughter's arm and took her triumphantly on the three-and-a-half-minute walk down the red carpet of the nave. Prince Charles turned and smiled encouragingly.

The glorious ritual with fanfares and voluntaries, choirboys and music of the highest order went on with flawless precision. The two young people at the heart of it all were the ones who added the much needed human touch. When it came to the vows Diana, with a hint of nerves, mixed up the order of her husband's long string of names and Charles, as though in sympathy, made a mistake in repeating his pledges, missing out the 'worldly' from the goods which he promised to share with her. Outside in the packed streets and squares crowds listening to the service on their transistors cheered loudly at each 'I will.'

A tumultuous reception greeted the couple as they emerged

from the West Door of St Paul's shortly after midday and the sound of cheering and church bells filled the air over London. Prince Charles, handsome in full naval uniform, grinned as thousands chanted, 'We want Charlie! We want Di!' The royal family made their traditional appearance on the balcony. The crowds went wild when Charles, egged on by Prince Andrew, turned and gave his bride a kiss. Then followed the wedding breakfast at which an hexagonal cake five feet high, made by the Royal Navy's Cookery School, H.M.S. *Pembroke* at Chatham, was cut and distributed.

At 4.20 p.m. thousands who had lingered, not wanting the day to end, were rewarded by the sight of the Prince and Princess of Wales leaving for their honeymoon in an open landau, smothered with confetti and trailing bunches of blue and silver balloons. Someone had scrawled 'Just Married' on the back of the vehicle. Now thoroughly relaxed and radiantly happy, the bride looked prettier than ever in rose-pink silk and a feathered tricorne hat.

They spent the night at Broadlands, the family home of the Mountbattens where the Queen and Prince Philip had stayed on the first week of their honeymoon. Privacy and the chance to be alone together lay ahead. They flew from Southampton to Gibraltar in an Andover of the Queen's Flight to join the Royal Yacht *Britannia*. For the next few weeks, while they cruised the Mediterranean, photographers only caught glimpses of them on the deck of the *Britannia* but the photographs they took showed a couple suntanned, wonderfully happy and obviously in love.

Since then Prince Charles and his 'very special' girl have become probably the most sought-after and admired young couple in the world. The births of their two sons, Prince William and Prince Harry, have only served to endear them still more to a public which never seems to tire of hearing about them and the lives they lead. The sight of Prince Charles carefully negotiating the steps leading down from an aeroplane with a carrycot soon made it clear that he intended to be an involved and thoroughly modern father. Princess Diana, gradually achieving a very individual royal style of her own, shed the last vestiges of plumpness to become a slender, elegant young woman with the sort of dazzle one usually associates with film stars. These days she looks stunning in the eye of the camera whether appearing in casual clothes with a baby in her arms or making a grand entrance at a formal occasion in ballgown and jewels. The glamorous image, however, has proved to be only half the story. People have discovered she has a warm, understanding personality and a winning way with children and the old. The Prince, joking about his wife's overwhelming popularity on their visit to Australia, said wryly to a crowd shouting for 'Di' when only he was available, 'I'm terribly sorry, but I've only got one of her!'

# King Hussein
## —AND—
# Lisa Halaby

**E**ver since he ascended the throne of Jordan at the tender age of sixteen, the life of King Hussein has been riddled with danger, political intrigue and disaster. He has been shot at more times than he can remember, survived several attempts to prise him from his throne and been forced to tread a tightrope in turbulent Middle East politics. His courage in facing up to all these things has never been questioned.

One fateful day in February 1977, however, it looked as though life had dealt him one blow too many when his young queen, Alia, was killed in a helicopter crash on the approach to Amman. For the first time Hussein began to talk as though the fates were against him. Suddenly he looked older than his forty-two years. He sank into a deep melancholy that made his friends despair. His personal life in ruins, his young children motherless, he seemed to lose interest in everything.

No one then would have dared forecast that by the summer of the following year Hussein would have regained his old heroic spark, once more dashing around in fast cars, piloting his own jets and taking on all adversaries. But then, nobody knew that the arab king was about to meet the most important love of his life.

Hussein was rescued from his despair by a beautiful, honey-blonde American girl called Lisa Halaby. When he made her his queen in June 1978 he changed her name to Noor al Hussein, 'The Light of Hussein', because, he said, she had indeed been like a ray of light when she came into his life at his darkest hour.

On the face of it, the likelihood of their meeting in the first place seemed very remote. They came from entirely different cultures. She was an Ivy League beauty, a product of top-drawer America who joined the ranks of the rebellious young in the Sixties. He was a true prince of the desert, a young monarch whose roots went back into far history and who had been familiar with violence and tragedy from his earliest years. But though their lives started far apart, fate was all the time pulling the strings that would bring them together.

Hussein was born in Amman, the Jordanian capital, on 14 November 1935 when his grandfather, King Abdullah, was on the throne. From childhood he was taught that his most important mission in life was to ensure the continuance of the Hashemite dynasty, the ancient family to which he belonged, said to descend in a direct line from the Prophet, Mohammed. Both his parents were Hashemite. His father, Talal, was a gentle, cultured man despised by the hawk-like Abdullah because he made it plain that he had no ambition to take over the throne. His mother, Queen Zein, on the other hand, was a strong personality who involved herself deeply in the politics of the Middle East.

Young Hussein revered his grandfather, who had led the Arabs in their struggle to free themselves from Turkish domination and in 1920 founded the small kingdom of Transjordan, later simply called Jordan, but his childhood was undoubtedly overshadowed by the enmity between Abdullah and Talal. As a boy Hussein was quiet, contemplative, sensitive, with a soft-spoken courtesy that still accounts for a great deal of his charm today. His favourite subject at school was Arabic poetry. Abdullah, however, also detected a remarkable strength of character and set all his hopes on his grandson.

The young prince was sent away to be educated and prepared for the throne at Victoria College, a British public school in the Egyptian city of Alexandria. Far from hating it, as he expected, Hussein thrived on the somewhat spartan regime and welcomed the comradeship that public-school life brought him. To his joy he also disovered football and cricket. 'He did not excel at games,' wrote Peter Snow in his biography of the king, 'but people noticed he had a grave determination to do his best. They began to notice he had courage above average.'

While still a boy, however, something happened that affected him very deeply. His gentle father Talal was overtaken by a mental illness which made him not only dangerous but murderous when he had a sudden seizure. Abdullah turned more and more to the young prince as his hope for the future. He told him that it was his God-given mission as a Hashemite to care for and protect the people of Jordan. He began to take the boy with him on official visits, to show him to the people as their future king.

Hussein was only fifteen and on holiday from school in the summer of 1950 when Abdullah asked him to accompany him on a visit to the great golden-domed Aqsa mosque in Jerusalem. The old King was about to enter to take part in morning prayers when an assassin stepped from the shadows and shot him at point-blank range through the head. He fell dying at his grandson's feet. For an instant everyone stood still. Then Hussein lunged forward as the murderer turned to escape. Seeing he was trapped, he turned and aimed a revolver straight at the young prince. The gun went off; a bullet struck Hussein's chest throwing him backwards, but he was unharmed. By some miracle it had ricocheted off one of his medals. It was his first close brush with death.

Though everyone knew Talal was not stable enough to rule, he was proclaimed king after Abdullah's death while Hussein was sent to England to finish his education at Harrow and Sandhurst. On one occasion when he was at home on holiday from school, Talal attacked him with a knife. The Jordanian parliament decided the time had come to ask him to stand down and allow Hussein to take the throne.

So, in 1952, the year in which Lisa Halaby was born into a luxurious, wealthy American family, her future husband was about to succeed to one of the most precarious thrones in the world and a life that demanded every ounce of the courage he possessed.

Lisa's father, Najeeb Halaby, one of the world's top airline executives and one-time president of Pan American World Airways, was her first link with the Middle East. He was the son of a Syrian immigrant. Lisa's blonde beauty was inherited from her Swedish mother, Doris Carlquist.

She loved her parents dearly but her father's passion for work meant they were constantly moving house from coast to coast and this gave her a sense of not belonging anywhere. Sometimes she longed for roots but when she grew up she copied the pattern of her childhood and hardly ever stayed in one place for a long time.

Tall and bronzed with a mane of glorious honey-gold hair and a devastating smile, Lisa Halaby broke plenty of hearts in her teens. She attended school in Washington D.C. while her father was chairman of the U.S. Federal Aviation Administration, then became one of the first women graduates at Princeton University, New Jersey, where she decided to study architecture.

She became a true child of the rebellious, swinging Sixties, the era of Vietnam and the songs of Bob Dylan. She was thoroughly emancipated, outspoken and independent; a cheerleader and a wonderful athlete. There were plenty of boyfriends and her family and friends thought she would probably marry a high-powered businessman like her father. She left college in her sophomore term and opted out for a year to study photography, earning her keep working as a waitress in Colorado's plush ski resort at Aspen. Most of the time she lived in faded jeans and T-shirts but when she went home it was to a luxurious Fifth Avenue apartment where the Kennedys and Rockefellers were often invited for dinner.

While Lisa Halaby was capturing the hearts of the young men of Princeton with her radiant smile, Hussein was already encountering disaster in his private life. When he was only nineteen he married for the first time. His mother, Queen Zein, had noticed that he was very fond of his cousin Dina, a great-grand-niece of Sherif Hussein of Mecca, and she encouraged the match. They first met in London while Dina was studying at Girton College, Cambridge. She was dark-eyed, gentle, deeply intelligent but had no love of outdoor life and certainly no desire to share Hussein's passion for motor-racing and flying. The one thing they had in common was a deep pride in their Hashemite blood. It was not a love-match but the young couple seemed happy enough with each other. They were married in Amman on 19 April 1955 and after their honeymoon went to live at Hussein's villa at Hummar just outside the capital. Hussein was overjoyed when Dina presented him with a daughter they called Aliyah but, nevertheless, the marriage foundered and finally collapsed after only eighteen months. The delicate-looking Dina was in fact a tough intellectual, strongly political and not at all the kind of wife Hussein wanted. He was looking for warm, human companionship, a woman who would share his interests and allow him to be master in his own house.

After his divorce from Dina in 1956 Hussein allowed his zest for adventure and romance free rein. He was now one of the world's most eligible royals and was often seen in the company of beautiful girls both in the Middle East and Europe. Though small in stature, the young king was attractive, with his dark eyes and wide, generous mouth, and he had the charisma that seems to hang about all men who live with danger.

Hussein often gave informal parties at his palace at Shuna in the Jordan valley where the dancing would go on through the night and guests would be served breakfast on the shores of the Dead Sea. There were many Europeans as well as Jordanians at these parties. One night an R.A.F. officer brought a pretty, nineteen-year-old English girl called Toni Gardiner, who was the daughter of Lt. Col. Walker Gardiner attached to the British Military Mission in Jordan. Hussein was attracted to her immediately and soon discovered that besides being extremely decorative she had many other virtues that he admired, including a good-natured outlook on life and common sense. Before long he had asked her to marry him, believing that she would give him the settled personal life which he desperately needed.

Those nearest the King strongly advised against the marriage and urged him to try to find an arab girl to be his queen. But Hussein would not listen. Toni Gardiner was deeply in love with him and became a Moslem, adopting the name Muna al Hussein, 'Hussein's wish'. They were married on 25 May 1961. Muna gladly set aside all claims to the title of queen and set about making a happy and comfortable home life. Within the next few years they had four children: Abdullah born in 1962, Feisal, and twin girls, Zeina and Aisha. Hussein's daughter by Dina also came to live with them.

For a time the marriage was successful and the difficulties everyone expected from Hussein taking an English wife never occurred. But if his private life had reached a peaceful plateau, his political life had certainly not. There was nothing but turmoil in the Middle East. His marriage came under very great strain during the 1967 war with Israel when he was seldom out of uniform and spent more time with his army than with his family. Years of tension followed and he was forced to travel everywhere with a bodyguard of Bedouin troops. To the outside world the throne of Jordan looked very insecure. Hussein's health suffered from the constant tension, and life for him and Princess Muna became more and more difficult. The fact that she wanted nothing to do with the public role of being Hussein's consort but preferred to remain quietly in the background looking after his home and children began to have adverse effects. In the end it was not enough; Princess Muna was seen more and more often on solitary shopping trips to London and eventually an announcement was made that the marriage had ended.

After their divorce the king reached out for happiness a third time, choosing as his bride a dark, elegant air hostess, the daughter of a Jordanian diplomat who became Queen Alia. They had very little time together before she was killed in a helicopter crash on the outskirts of Amman in 1977. This time Hussein was inconsolable, feeling that he was destined never to achieve lasting personal happiness.

Hussein was war-weary, world-weary and his hair was streaked with grey. Friends tried to rekindle his interest in all his old pursuits but he remained sunk in melancholy. Sometimes, however, he would drive out to Amman airport in order to fly for pleasure. And it was in the corridor at the airport that he first saw Lisa Halaby.

Ever since she graduated from Princeton, Lisa had drifted around the world never staying long anywhere. She regarded herself as 'a bit of a loner'. That part of her that acknowledged and was fascinated by her arab ancestry drew her to the Middle East, where she travelled extensively and began to study Arabic.

She first visited Jordan in 1975 to see her father who was in Amman as director of the Halaby International Corporation, a civil airline consultancy. The following year she returned to the Jordanian capital to work at the airport as a consultant architect and planner.

More than a year went by before she met Hussein. The King was often to be seen at the airport, for he enjoyed the company of fellow pilots and, whatever else happened, he was determined to put in enough flying hours to keep his pilot's licence. He was qualified to take up anything, including the big jets. They used to pass each other in the corridor as she hurried from office to office with sheafs of paper and architectural drawings. She noticed that his dark eyes were sad. He noticed her lovely smile.

At the beginning of 1978 Jordan was expecting the delivery of her first jumbo jet and a ceremony had been arranged at Amman airport. Hussein noticed the tall, golden-haired girl with the radiant smile among the waiting dignitaries, heard she was Najeeb Halaby's daughter and asked for her to be brought over and introduced to him. They laughed and talked together for a few minutes, then he resumed his social duties. But after that first meeting he could not get her out of his mind.

'The telephone rang one day and he asked me to help him with the plans for a house he was having built. There were some problems and he thought as I was an architect I could help him,' she told *The Tatler*. 'I didn't think I was properly qualified to deal with the problem he mentiond, but I agreed to help. It was really through putting our heads together over this problem of his house that we began to draw closer together.'

One evening Hussein asked her if she would dine with him. The former Princeton graduate replied that she would be honoured to accept His Majesty's invitation. After that they had dinner together every night for six weeks. 'Very spontaneously our friendship became something deeper, with no consideration for the consequences,' she laughed.

The King was delighted to discover they had a mutual love of the desert and outdoor life. She not only shared his interest in flying but could ski, ride, sail and play a fair game of tennis. For the first three months they met discreetly, trying to keep their courtship a secret, even from their families. But it soon became obvious to those closest to them in Amman that they were falling in love and that Lisa Halaby had worked a miracle as far as Hussein was concerned.

When the time came to face the world's press on the announcement of their intended marriage, the King made no bones about his feelings for the lovely American girl by his side. 'My life has been full of tragedy,' he admitted softly. 'She has brought me a strength and happiness I didn't believe possible to find again.' Even Lisa's father, obviously overjoyed at finding himself with a Hashemite king for a son-in-law, became positively lyrical. 'It is true love, of that I am certain,' he told anyone prepared to listen. 'My daughter admires the King, the strength of his convictions, his simplicity and courage.'

Their wedding took place in June 1978. The simple Islamic ceremony at which, according to the Koran, only men were allowed to be present and hear the vows, took place at Zahran Palace, the home of King Hussein's mother, in a flower-filled drawing-room set aside for the purpose. Though the ceremony was in every way arabic the bridegroom, who had grown a short beard, chose to wear a dark-blue Savile Row suit for the occasion. His twenty-six-year-old bride had ordered her white silk crêpe wedding gown from Paris. Her honey-coloured hair was held in place by a small coronet. She wore very little make-up on her smooth, ivory skin but flawless diamonds glittered in her ears and on her wrists.

The pair sat together on a small sofa in the centre of the room as the Chief Justice of the Islamic Court, Ibrahim Catan, began the simple ceremony, speaking in Arabic. Afterwards, observers said she glanced towards Hussein with a nervous smile and he leaned towards her as though to give her assurance. Looking into his face every few words she said in halting Arabic, 'I have betrothed myself to thee in marriage for the dowry agreed upon.' The King replied in his deep, soft voice: 'I have accepted you as my wife in marriage for the dowry agreed upon.' The Chief Justice then took a small book to the King who signed on the right-hand side of three different pages. The bride signed the three pages on the left and, looking up at her father, joked about how difficult it was signing her new name from right to left in arab fashion. It had taken four minutes to turn Lisa Halaby into Queen Noor.

Laughing and smiling, King Hussein and the 'Light' of his life walked on to a flower-filled terrace to face the world together, the beautiful young American seeming to take with ease to her new role as a Moslem. Many members of the diplomatic corps meeting her for the first time were enchanted by her warm sense of humour and her compassion. Hussein, they felt, had definitely picked a winner.

After the two-hour reception they slipped away to Aqaba, the Jordanian resort with its fabulous coral reef, for the first part of their honeymoon. Shortly afterwards they turned up in Britain, looking blissfully happy, the King explaining that he wanted to show Queen Noor the misty hills and glens of Scotland, which he loved so much.

Their days of freedom together were all too few. Fresh turbulence was brewing in the Middle East and they soon had to return to the sprawling royal palace on the hillside outside Amman where Queen Noor began to rebuild Hussein's life.

One of the first things she did was to suggest moving into a smaller palace which she could make into a real home. Then she gathered his eight children by his former wives together, doing everything she could to persuade them to accept her and to make their lives happy and secure. Since then she has given the King four more children to add to his Hashemite brood: the little Princes Hamzah and Hashem, the tiny Princess Iman, and Princess Raya born in February 1986.

When Noor first asked her husband how she could learn to be a queen he told her simply: 'Just be yourself', and she has followed his advice with triumphant results. Though an undeniably glamorous figure whether dressed in khaki uniform or Paris couture, she has no difficulty in communicating. She has learned to speak colloquial Arabic and feels herself that she has managed to bridge the culture gap. She does not become directly involved with politics but has found herself becoming deeply interested. When they are alone she and King Hussein spend a great deal of time discussing world affairs and the conditions in the Middle East. He listens carefully to what she has to say. In every day life, however, she likes to concentrate her efforts on trying to improve the lives of ordinary people in any way in which she thinks she can bring her influence to bear. One of her pet projects, for instance, is the Queen Noor Scheme for the Greening and Development of Villages. She is especially concerned with the place of women in arab society and has been quoted as saying, 'Women are not subservient in Islam. They used to lead the battles and were great poets and the possibilities for women in Islam are immense. We have to make sure we use our potential.' She is often to be seen squatting on her heels in the dust of a Jordan village, talking to the women as they weave, asking them about their children and looking thoroughly at ease dressed in a simple shirt and jodhpurs. Being queen of a desert kingdom has meant considerable personal adjustment. Before her marriage she had always been an independent girl who liked nothing better than to travel and to be able to move freely from place to place. That was why she loved airports. Being Queen of

Jordan has meant, of necessity, that she has had to accept certain restrictions. For instance, there is always a bodyguard hovering somewhere in the background. She complains with some amusement that she has found it impossible to go out and jog because there would always be someone jogging along behind her. Sometimes in the early days of her marriage she had the occasional twinge of loneliness, missing not having a close friend to confide in. She was delighted when her father flew into Amman in his private plane to see her for a short visit and delighted when American friends turned up unexpectedly.

Being American in a volatile Middle East country could have produced considerable problems. For instance, in the days after the American raid on the Libyan capital of Tripoli in 1986 there were rowdy demonstrations outside the U.S. Embassy in Amman and the anti-American feeling was strong. But Queen Noor went through it all calmly. She says she does not feel American any longer, nor is she regarded as such in arab countries. Just the same, security around her is tight and her bodyguards show alarm when she forgets who she is and acts on impulse. 'I love and owe America a good deal,' she told the *New York Times*, 'but Jordan is my country now.'

Her schedule is tight but she always makes time for the children, whether her own or those from her husband's former marriages. She spent a lot of time on her own as a child and now enjoys having young ones around her, planning parties for them, reading to them and watching them play together in the palace gardens.

King Hussein soon realized that he had not only gained a beautiful consort but an ally and a wonderful envoy, especially in his tricky dealings with America. Queen Noor's smile and personality often brings results more quickly than the work of half a dozen diplomats!

After the affairs of state are over it is said they are still like a young couple in love. He teases her about her Bruce Springsteen records and the exercises she performs to rock-and-roll music. They laugh a lot together. He admires the way she handles her Mercedes in the winding streets of Amman and her skill at the wheel of the family's yellow speedboat. She in turn is fascinated by his political understanding and amused by his dry humour.

They now live in a fine sandstone palace in Amman which has

a cool, marble-floored interior. The rooms are resplendent with silver and mother-of-pearl with rose-red walls and long, low couches. At splendid state dinners she sits beside the King, glittering with diamonds, in a dining-room lined and roofed with silk like a magnificent Bedouin tent.

Queen Noor shares the danger line that Hussein walks like a tightrope but when asked how she feels about that aspect of her life she replies like a true daughter of Islam: 'The King is a fatalist and so am I. We are very alike in some ways.'

# Princess Beatrix
## —AND—
# Claus von Amsberg

There has never been a royal wedding quite like that of Crown Princess Beatrix of The Netherlands and Claus von Amsberg of Bonn. The golden wedding coach was pelted with smoke-bombs, anti-German leaflets rained down upon the procession, a thousand demonstrators chanted, '*Claus raus!*' (Claus out!) and steel-helmeted police charged in with batons. Throughout the fracas Beatrix, outwardly calm and smiling bravely, clasped the hand of the man she had defied everyone to marry.

Their marriage reflected the agonizing conflict between love and duty. The Dutch people, who suffered bitterly at the hands of the Germans during the last war, were appalled when they heard that Queen Juliana's daughter, Crown Princess Beatrix, heir to the throne, was planning to marry a German diplomat who had been in Hitler's army. But the determined – some said wilful – Princess was deeply in love and would have no one else. In the end even Queen Juliana, who opposed the match, had to say that Claus von Amsberg was 'obviously the choice of her heart'.

Time has mellowed the feelings that were rampant on that wedding day. Beatrix, now Queen, has become respected and admired, both as monarch and wife and mother. Prince Claus, as he is now called, has shown himself to be a sensitive, likable man. He soon learned to write and speak Dutch fluently, devoting himself to social work of many kinds. Eventually the Dutch people forgave him for being German when he gave Beatrix the first male heir for the House of Orange for nearly a century.

Only a woman as strong-willed as Beatrix could have had the courage and nerve to go through with the sort of ordeal she faced on her wedding day. But then, she had always been a Princess who knew what she wanted and usually got it. She is the eldest daughter of Queen Juliana and Prince Bernhard, himself German born, as Beatrix reminded her mother when she tried to dissuade her from marrying Claus.

From the very beginning her life was always accompanied by dramatic events. She was born on 31 January 1938 just after her father had missed death by inches in a near-fatal motoring accident. The cannons boomed out fifty-one times to tell The Netherlands that a female heir to the throne had arrived. She was christened Beatrix Wilhelmina Armgard at St Jacobskerk in The Hague. The royal family rode to her christening in a golden coach and there were cheering throngs of well-wishers.

Beatrix was treated with ultra-scrupulous care as a baby. The motherly Queen Juliana took pride in supervising the housework at Soestdijk Palace and kept a close eye on her precious baby. If a toy or rattle fell to the floor in the pristine nursery, it was immediately sterilized. When it was time for the tiny Princess to be fed, a footman would arrive with a few spoonfuls of hot oatmeal served on a huge silver tray with a cover. In spite of this smothering, 'Trix', as the family called her, developed a distinct personality by the time she was eighteen months old.

Her early life was dominated by the fact that the Germans invaded The Netherlands in May 1940. The Dutch royal family were spirited away in an English destroyer and for a time lived in a house in Gloucestershire loaned to them by Lord Bledisloe. Then Juliana agreed to go to Canada with her children while her mother, Queen Wilhelmina, stayed in England with Prince Bernhard. This meant that Beatrix's early years were spent not only far from her native land but cut off from her father for most of the time. Her first memories were of a nursery school in Ottawa. She was seven and a half when she first saw her own country after the war.

Her later childhood was more settled but still fraught with crises. In September 1945 Juliana, not wanting to appear old-fashioned, enrolled Beatrix and her younger sister, Princess Irene, in a progressive school run by a former anarchist called Boeke. They were taken to class in a chauffeured limousine with two detectives. A row broke out when it became known that they were being 'exposed' to the influence of Boeke. Prince Bernhard, who favoured a more formal education, found that, while his daughters were making great headway in painting and sculpture, they were far behind on academic subjects. He had them removed and they went to a school in the village of Baarn where they completed their secondary education with excellent results.

Princess Beatrix always had a reputation for being a bit precocious. She signed herself 'Trix of Orange.' Once she asked her governess, 'We are rich, aren't we?' To which the governess replied, 'Yes, you are.' Beatrix, grinning, told her, 'Well, I can't say I'm sorry.'

She inherited a great deal of her wit and sharp humour from Prince Bernhard. 'Beatrix had always been more attracted to her dashing father than to her rather plain, very religious mother,' wrote William Hoffman in his biography of Juliana.

Princess Beatrix's schooldays were overshadowed by the tragic blindness of her youngest sister, Marijke, who had been born with cataracts on both eyes two years after their return from Canada. Operations had only restored minimal sight to one eye. Juliana was distraught. She had succeeded to the throne after her mother, Queen Wilhelmina, abdicated in 1948 but became obsessed with the necessity of finding a cure for her child and precipitated a national crisis by engaging a faith healer, Greet Hofmans, who came to have great influence over the Queen. The mystic moved into Soestdijk Palace in The Hague and more or less took over the household. After two years of her overpowering presence Prince Bernhard lost his temper and threw her out.

The crisis passed, however, and Juliana remained secure in the affection of the Dutch people. They loved her for her simplicity and warm-heartedness and readily forgave her peccadillos. She became, however, increasingly drawn towards mysticism. At one time she gave a great deal of attention to a man called George Adamski, a sixty-year-old former California hamburger-stand operator who founded a Temple of Scientific Philosophy. She also listened raptly to the adventures of a flying saucer expert who claimed he had met spacemen from Venus while on a picnic in the Arizona desert. The down-to-earth Beatrix showed impatience with her mother's credulity.

In spite of everything the family had very happy times. Both Juliana and Bernhard encouraged their daughters to take up riding, skiing and sailing. Each year at the annual regatta at

Friesland the Princesses Beatrix, Irene and Margriet, and eventually the plucky little Marijke, could be seen happily crewing for their father.

By the time she was sixteen Beatrix showed a distinct taste for fashionable clothes and expensive jewellery, but her mother had no intention of letting her socialize with young men. She was very strict and very aware that she was raising a future queen. Beatrix had every intention of being a well-informed, modern monarch when she came to the throne. At the University of Leyden she studied legal science, parliamentary history, political science and sociology, and emerged with a distinction. She celebrated her graduation on board her yacht *Green Dragon*, which the Dutch people had given her for her eighteenth birthday, when she was confirmed as a member of the Dutch Reformed Church and installed as a Councillor of State. She was now in a position to take over the throne if Queen Juliana decided to abdicate. This began to be thought likely in 1961 when Juliana was approaching her twenty-fifth wedding anniversary. Her marriage was described as 'very shaky' but she confounded the pessimists and celebrated her silver wedding with one of the most lavish parties Holland has ever seen, inviting all the royalty of Europe for a night to be remembered aboard the luxury liner *Oranje*.

As Crown Princess, Beatrix travelled extensively in Europe, the Middle East, Japan and China. She even turned up in the Soviet Union without telling anyone she intended to make the trip. It was becoming clear that Princess Beatrix was not the sort of person who welcomed being told what to do. To her mother's horror she once went on a tour of the red-light district of Amsterdam in the company of a Salvation Army officer, because she wanted to see for herself. She was sometimes accused of being abrupt and haughty. But she also picked up the title of 'The Laughing Princess' because she had a good sense of humour. Even on official occasions laughter sometimes broke in. Once, when she had been invited to launch a ship the champagne drenched her instead of the hull. There was a moment's silence, then she collapsed in a fit of giggles.

By the time she reached her twenties Beatrix was a very attractive girl in a typically Dutch way – fresh, rounded, with soft golden hair and blue eyes. She was one of the most eligible princesses in Europe but showed no signs of wanting to be married. When she was twenty-four gossip spread about the fact that she was being escorted regularly by a twenty-five-year-old lawyer called Bob Steensma. A party was given at the palace to which he was invited and it was thought at the time that it was intended to introduce Steensma to society and foreign royals as Beatrix's future consort. But Mr Steensma disappeared into the mists of time.

With her daughters reaching marriageable age, Queen Juliana had naturally hoped they would all find titled, personable, suitable young men. But she had already had a crisis of major proportions. Beatrix's younger sister Princess Irene had caused uproar in Holland by marrying Prince Carlos Hugo of Bourbon Parma, a claimant to the Spanish throne and a fascist supporter of Franco. Though Juliana tried to stop the wedding, for it was considered politically disastrous, Irene married Carlos Hugo in Rome on 29 April 1964. None of her family was present. The affair was considered to have been a serious threat to the throne but the Queen weathered it.

Meanwhile informal discussions were being held about finding a suitable consort for Princess Beatrix. There was some understanding that she might choose Prince Richard ze Sayn Wittgenstein-Berleburg. The two families had considered the matter and the Prince and Beatrix had agreed to meet.

Arrangements were duly made so that the couple could spend a well-chaperoned sporting holiday together in the Swiss skiing resort of Gstaad. A large, well-furnished chalet was found and Beatrix was driven to Gstaad by her chauffeur. Prince Richard got a lift: he arrived in a blue Porsche driven by his best friend, who had already booked himself into a local hotel. His friend was Claus von Amsberg.

Claus, who worked for the West German Foreign Service in Bonn, was a handsome man, blue-eyed, square-sholdered, with the polish of a career diplomat. The three of them went skiing together but after only a few days it was obvious that Beatrix found the Prince's friend very attractive. At the end of the holiday Prince Richard went home and Claus accompanied Beatrix back to Holland.

Juliana was appalled when she realized that her daughter, heir to the throne, had fallen in love with a thirty-eight-year-old

German diplomat who had been a member of the Hitler Youth and served in the Wehrmacht. Claus was a totally unexpected suitor. She made frantic attempts to have him posted to some far-flung outpost, but to no avail. Her objection was purely political. Frantic efforts were made to investigate his background. It was discovered that he had been born on 6 September 1926 in the German country town of Dotzingen. His family were minor aristocrats, his mother being Baroness von dem Bussche-Haddenhausen. His father had emigrated to Tanganyika (now Tanzania) in 1928 and Claus had been brought up on the coffee and sisal plantation where his father was estate manager. He was sent back to Germany to be educated at Hamburg University at an unfortunate time. It was 1938, and Europe was beginning to dread the sound of the German jackboot. Claus von Amsberg became a member of the Hitler Youth. He had not, he pointed out, any choice. It was compulsory, almost automatic. He was not old enough to be called up for military service until 1944 and was then sent to Italy with the 90th Panzer Division. He was captured by the Americans in 1945 having seen hardly any action.

As the war ended he was transferred to a P.O.W. camp near Amersham, Buckinghamshire, in England. His proficiency in languages earned him the job of camp interpreter. His proficiency at bridge became an even greater asset, for the American camp commander was a keen player.

With wartime resentment in Holland still deep, it was considered of prime importance to check his wartime career. Nothing against him could be found. He was never a member of the Nazi party. When the Dutch government checked with East Germany and the Soviet Union to see if there were any outstanding charges against him, the result was negative: none existed.

Claus joined the diplomatic service after the war and in his work as economics attaché for the Ministry of Foreign Affairs in Bonn he visited almost every African nation. He was at one time third secretary at the German Embassy in the Dominican Republic. When he met Princess Beatrix he was living in a bachelor apartment in Bonn, his leisure time taken up with books, music, playing golf and tennis, and water skiing, his favourite sport.

During the tense year before they married he was wise enough not to say anything that would aggravate the situation. Few people knew how hard Juliana tried to prevent the wedding, even contacting the Foreign Minister in Bonn and attempting to get Claus transferred out of Europe. When Beatrix heard what her mother was up to, she went on a three-day hunger strike. Juliana was so worried about her daughter that she gave in.

The first indication to the general public in Holland that Crown Princess Beatrix was in love came with a photograph of her walking with Claus in the palace gardens. It was snatched by a photographer hiding in the shrubbery. Official silence was broken in May 1965 when a government spokesman said they were 'just good friends'.

Early in July 1965 the Queen herself appeared on nationwide radio and TV to announce the engagement of twenty-seven-year-old Beatrix to Claus Georg Wilhelm Otto Friedrich Gerd von Amsberg. 'I assure you, it is a good thing,' said Juliana, speaking from Soestdijk Palace. But her sentiments were not shared by the Dutch people, who felt outraged that a man who had worn German uniform would eventually be consort to their future queen. Soon there were demonstrations in the streets, rallies, marches and cries of, '*Claus, raus!*'

To the Dutch it seemed incredible that Juliana should permit such a marriage after the *débâcle* over Princess Irene marrying a fascist. This engagement was much more significant since Beatrix was next in line to the throne and heiress to a fortune. Sections of the press went so far as to suggest that, since Irene had given up her right to the throne, Beatrix should do the same. The outcome of such an action would have been disastrous to the House of Orange, for neither of the other two daughters of Juliana and Bernhard would have been able to take on the burden of the Crown, Margriet having put herself beyond the pale, as far as the aristocrats were concerned, by marrying an 'unsuitable' commoner and Marijke being, by sad misfortune, partially blind.

Prince Bernhard, who became a close supporter of Claus, said in an interview on the subject of his daughters' rather controversial marriages, 'The time of arranging a marriage is past. My wife and I don't believe in it at all. If it's going to be a marriage that brings lasting happiness, it's got to come about naturally.'

Claus, it appears, had more doubts about going through with the wedding than Beatrix because he could see that his past, though it was without dishonour, might endanger her future. But his feelings for her were as strong as hers for him and their doubts were resolved. They decided to face it out.

Juliana encouraged them to appear together on television and before the press. The decision paid dividends. The Dutch peered intently at their screens as Claus von Amsberg came before them for the first time. He was handsome certainly, but also cheerful, modest, and nothing like the sort of German they had in mind. He tried to answer with honesty the difficult questions thrown at him. He quietly explained that he was deeply in love with Beatrix, that he was sorry about his past and that it was his most fervent wish to be accepted by the Dutch people. He was obviously sincere. 'The press conference was a brave gesture,' wrote Queen Juliana's biographer, William Hoffman. 'The Dutch royal family were not given to meeting the press and afterwards some of the more moderate elements in the country seemed willing to forgive Claus his past and give the marriage a chance.' Beatrix, too, came over well. When asked what she thought about the demonstrations she replied, 'It is much healthier for people to speak their minds than to bottle up their feelings.' She had always been reserved about expressing her emotions, said her father, and he was touched to see her sitting hand-in-hand with Claus being grilled before the TV cameras.

Just as things seemed to be calming down a little, Princess Beatrix dropped another bombshell. She announced that she would be married in Amsterdam instead of The Hague. This ignored Dutch royal tradition which, apparantly, requires a monarch or future monarch to be married in The Hague, inaugurated in Amsterdam and buried at Delft. Juliana immediately opposed the suggestion. She knew how much Amsterdam had suffered at the hands of the Germans and how the memory of Anne Frank and thousands of other innocent victims had left bitter feelings. But Beatrix saw things another way. 'If I win the hearts of the Amsterdammers,' she declared, 'I will win the hearts of all The Netherlands.'

The States General still had to approve the marriage if Beatrix was to remain in line for the throne. The debate was seen on national television and one legislator even went so far as to say he felt sorry for Claus. He seemed a decent enough fellow, he admitted, but should be disqualified for the same reason a crippled man could not take part in a professional sport. Nevertheless, the States General did not want to bring down the House of Orange and finally the vote was 132–9 in Beatrix's favour.

So, love had its way. The wedding day, 10 March 1966, dawned grey and cold with a promise of rain in the air. The Dam square, before the palace in Amsterdam, was full but far from overcrowded. The four-mile length of the route was lined with spectators but there was plenty of room for more. There had been a noisy march on the palace early in the day and both Princess Beatrix and Claus knew that their reception would be largely hostile but nevertheless they were determined to face it as cheerfully as possible.

At 10.10 precisely the gates of the palace opened and the wedding procession began. The police were standing facing towards the crowds, instead of the procession, to enable them to spot trouble-makers. Three large police trucks packed with men tagged along behind the coaches and limousines. The reason was that, by now, every youthful demonstrator in Holland had arrived in Amsterdam and the police were expecting chaos. Besides the 'Provos', as they were called, everybody else came out on to the streets and demonstrated that day, including the local anarchists and republicans.

Princess Beatrix and Claus travelled together to their wedding in a magnificent gold coach. Both were smiling bravely. They had been warned there would be trouble, and there was. Five smoke-bombs had exploded outside the palace before dawn, now they were being thrown under the feet of the horses, which tossed their heads as the smoke-bombs burst around them and the coachman, holding on for all he was worth, obviously feared they were going to bolt. The eight footmen riding outside the coach were almost blinded by acrid fumes. The coach emerged from a drifting pall of smoke to reveal Beatrix, still smiling. Cheers were beginning to be heard above the rest of the din. She seemed oblivious of the leaflets that were being thrown at the coach from all directions. Claus tried to smile but showed his tension, especially when a live chicken daubed with a swastika was released into the *mêlée*.

Despite everything the old city was a perfect setting, with its narrow streets, its canals, its gabled merchant houses. The golden coach, presented in 1898 by the city of Amsterdam to Queen

Wilhelmina, made a glittering contrast to the city's sombre colours as it wound its way through the streets and over the bridges. Horsemen carrying banners and detachments of cavalry added to the pageantry.

They drove first to the City Hall where the civil ceremony was held in a room banked with spring flowers. The only time Beatrix came near to tears was not when the smoke-bombs were exploding round her but when Amsterdam's Mayor, Gijs von Hall, reminded her of how she and Claus came from 'different milieux, which involved a whole complex of different characteristics, interests, desires and ideals'.

The religious ceremony was held at Amsterdam's Westerkerk and by now loyal supporters were also out in the streets and cheering. One reporter watching the Princess step down from the coach wrote, 'She looked astonishingly beautiful. I believe it must be true that love transforms.' The Dutch princesses, it was true, had never been noted beauties but Beatrix, holding on to the arm of her Claus, was beautiful that day. She was wearing a dress of white satin, simply cut, with a train appliquéd with white velvet, a full tulle veil and a tiara of diamonds and pearls that had first been worn by Queen Wilhelmina in 1900.

Few of the crowned heads of Europe had accepted invitations to the wedding, fearing some kind of trouble, but among those who looked on as the couple stood at the altar to take their vows were Princess Alexandra and Princess Marina from Britain, the King of the Belgians and the King of Greece, the Grand Duchess of Luxembourg and the Aga Khan in all their wedding finery. The text read by the minister of the Dutch Reformed Church reminded Beatrix that 'there is nothing love cannot face'.

As they emerged from the church, for once the cheering of their supporters seemed to drown out the more discordant noises, and Claus, looking less tense, volunteered a wave and a smile. Beatrix, laughing and smiling on her husband's arm, seemed to diffuse the hostility. Afterwards they appeared on the palace balcony, which was decorated with thousands of pale-yellow tulips. The crowd below numbered only about two thousand but, obviously deciding the newlyweds had had enough opposition for one day, they cheered, and there were even some shouts of 'Good luck.' John Grigg of *The Observer* had the last word for the whole fantastic day: 'It was a rowdy affair, though it might have been far worse.'

Before they left for their honeymoon Prince Claus, as he was now to be known, recorded a brief address to the Dutch people: 'I know that some of you cannot be reconciled to our wedding. I can assure you that I have understanding for this. I know that during the last war much suffering and injustice was caused. ...'

Prince Bernhard arranged their secret honeymoon destination. He promised it would take the world five days to find them. Later it was disclosed that they were staying on the island of Cozumel off the Mexican coast. They were protected by Mexican troops, armed police and Dutch detectives. They stayed in a villa lent to them by the former President of Mexico, Adolfo Lopez Mateos, and spent most of the time sunbathing on the patio or swimming and spear-fishing from the President's fast motor-cruiser. Before returning to Holland they went on safari in Tanzania.

Things were much calmer on their return. Many people were, in fact, rather ashamed of the demonstrations at Beatrix's wedding, blamed them on the lunatic fringe and the 'Provos' but nevertheless were secretly glad that someone had protested on their behalf. In spite of the hostility, however, thousands of people contributed to a cheque for £100,000 which was presented to Princess Beatrix as a wedding present. She announced that the cheque would be donated to charity.

As Hoffman points out in his biography of Juliana, though the marriage of Beatrix and Claus produced the greatest outcry against the monarchy in The Netherlands since the attempted socialist take-over in 1918, Queen Juliana was not personally threatened as she had been in the Greet Hofmans episode, the George Adamski affair or over Princess Irene's unpopular marriage to Carlos Hugo. 'Each of these incidents prompted demands that she abdicate in favour of Beatrix but no one called for her abdication after her daughter's marriage to Claus von Amsberg.' There was a general feeling in Holland that the Queen had been given a rough ride by her wilful daughters. She had tried to bring them up in a modern fashion and they had given her nothing but headaches. The only danger for Juliana after Beatrix married Claus was that sentiment in The Netherlands might swing towards abolition of the monarchy altogether. The Dutch government soon calmed Juliana's fears in this respect in the summer of 1966 by making her the highest-paid crowned head in Europe.

Their first home together was a small *château* called Drakensteyn near the palace where Queen Juliana continued to live. Beatrix had bought it with her own money and furnished it to her own taste. It had twenty rooms and a moat. Prince Claus gradually became accepted. In fact, he became a great asset to the royal family. He involved himself in social work and development aid which brought him into touch with ordinary people. Once his Dutch was fluent he made it his business to learn the colloquial language of the workers so that his approach could be as friendly as possible.

Nothing, however, could have sealed Prince Claus's final acceptance more than the event that took place on 27 April 1967. Beatrix gave birth to an eight-pound six-ounce baby boy, Willem Alexander. Juliana was at her daughter's side when the baby was born at University Hospital, Utrecht. For the first time in nearly a century The Netherlands had a Prince of Orange and a male heir to the Dutch throne. The country went crazy. People cheered themselves hoarse, a 101-gun salute was fired and Claus was at last forgiven for being a German. Church bells rang out over the tulip fields and Beatrix, holding her baby son, laughed for joy. Ten thousand people signed a register of congratulations at Soestdijk Palace and presents poured in when Beatrix returned to Drakensteyn. When news of the birth was conveyed to the conductor of Holland's famous Concertgebouw Orchestra, then in New York, the performance was stopped so that the Dutch national anthem could be played.

Willem-Alexander was named after one of the sons of William III, Queen Wilhelmina's father, who did not live long enough to succeed to the throne. The choice of name proved very popular with the Dutch people. Prince Bernhard was told the good news while he was acting as host at a party being given for the King and Queen of Nepal. When informed by an aide that he had become the grandfather of a baby boy and that both mother and child were doing well, he raised his glass and cried out, 'He's here! It's a son.' After receiving heartiest congratulations from everyone present he rushed to the royal palace in Amsterdam to appear before cheering crowds on the balcony alongside Queen Juliana. The Dutch were relieved to see Juliana and Bernhard appearing together in such happy circumstances after so many rumours about the state of their marriage. Beatrix and Claus, they felt, had to be thanked for that, too.

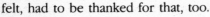

When they finally appeared together to show off their son to the world their own happiness seemed infectious. Only the hard core of youthful rebels and anti-monarchists held out against the pleasant picture of a beaming Princess Beatrix, proud Prince Claus and robust heir to the throne.

A new phase in the lives of Beatrix and Claus came in April 1980 when Juliana decided to abdicate and Beatrix became Queen of The Netherlands. The years between have not been without their problems. Prince Claus was seriously ill for two years, but recovered. They now have three sturdy teenage sons and the future of the House of Orange seems secure, more secure than anyone would have believed on that incredible day in 1966.

# King Constantine
## —AND—
# Princess Anne-Marie

At the magnificent reception which followed his sister Sophia's wedding to the future King Juan Carlos of Spain, the handsome young Crown Prince Constantine of Greece paid attention to only one girl. He danced every dance with her, never left her side. Now and then his mother, Queen Frederika, would drift up to him, take his arm and whisper fiercely, 'Tino, will you please look after the other girls.' But next time she caught sight of him it was with the same lovely partner. 'I'm sorry,' Constantine told his mother, 'but I don't want anybody else to get the same idea about Anne-Marie as I have.'

It had been like that ever since Constantine and the princess from Denmark first became aware of each other. Anne-Marie was then only fourteen, but the Crown Prince knew she was the love of his life and simply waited for her to grow up. He offered her a crown, she became the youngest queen in the world but the greatest test of their love came when the crown was snatched from them in what became known as the coup of the Greek colonels and the young couple had to fly from Greece into exile.

Their story really began at the circus in Copenhagen when Princess Anne-Marie was twelve years old. The Greek royal family were paying a visit to Denmark and one night it was decided to send all the young people to see the clowns. Anne-Marie, the youngest daughter of King Frederik and Queen Ingrid, was already an exceptionally pretty girl with a delightful, shy manner. Crown Prince Constantine, her third cousin, was dark, handsome, athletic, and she later admitted to friends, 'I adored him from that moment on.' At that time, however, the teenage Tino had his mind more on yachting and karate and did not pay much attention to the pretty schoolgirl. His father King Paul did, however. With uncanny foresight he said to his wife Queen Frederika, 'Look, she is like a butterfly. I hope Tino will marry her one day.' Two years later, when Anne-Marie was fourteen, they met again and this time both of them realized they were meant for each other.

The Greeks and the Danes seem to have a special affinity. The people of Athens have a saying: 'Danes make good Greeks', for their own King George I, an exceptionally successful monarch, was originally from the Danish royal family.

Durable and democratic, the royal house to which Princess Anne-Marie belongs is the oldest in Europe. Her birth at Amalienborg Palace, Copenhagen in August 1946 brought great joy to King Frederick and Queen Ingrid and to a Denmark only recently liberated from the horrors of war. There was a strong English influence in her upbringing, for her nurse was Mary North, daughter of Admiral Sir Dudley North. She began her education at a kindergarten not far from the palace. When she was seven she was sent to an ordinary girls' high school just outside Copenhagen. The bicycle-riding Danish royal family are famous for their natural, democratic way of life and did not intend to make an exception with Anne-Marie. She was allowed to wander freely through the streets of Copenhagen, go shopping and take holidays with her friends, many of them the daughters of undistinguished middle-class parents. She earned her pocket-money by asking family friends if they wanted their cars washed. Her allowance was modest and she usually spent it on ice cream and sweets, which she shared out generously.

All the more surprising, then, was the decision to break the family tradition and send the youngest princess to a fashionable finishing school in Switzerland. Her elder sisters, Princess Margarethe, destined to become Queen of Denmark, and Princess Benedikte, were sent to English girls' schools but for some reason it was decided that Anne-Marie should be 'finished' at a more sophisticated establishment, and the Chatelard School, 3,000 feet above Montreux in Switzerland, was chosen. Anne-Marie did not want to go and Queen Ingrid found herself flying to Switzerland twice during the first term to encourage her homesick daughter. Once she had settled down Princess Anne-Marie proved to be extremely popular and made many friends. She mixed well and had all the normal interests including 'rock' music and sewing. She had excellent taste in clothes but not a great deal of money to spend on them. Friends who were at school with her said she preferred to let one of them wash and set her sleek hair rather than go to the village hairdresser, where everyone knew who she was, and stared.

At home in Denmark the English influence continued, for the King and Queen made a point of seeing that there were always two or three young English girls as companions for their daughters so that by constantly speaking English the three princesses became fluent.

Just how lovely the youngest Danish princess had become was seen by everybody at her first big party – equivalent to the English debutante's 'coming out' – held in the ballroom of the palace, for this special night draped with cloth of gold and decorated with orchids. Anne-Marie, waltzing under the great chandeliers, was the focus of all eyes. She had dressed for the ball in her bedroom overlooking an ancient, cobbled courtyard where sentries in blue and white uniform stood to attention. Excited, eager, she put on her first off-the-shoulder gown, her smooth hair gleaming under the lights. There was no doubt: she was grown-up enough now for Tino.

Though Prince Constantine's name had been linked with several eligible princesses and beautiful actresses as he emerged as a very personable, energetic young man, there was never really anyone but Anne-Marie from the beginning. He visited Denmark when she was fourteen and this time the attraction was mutual. 'We took one look at each other and that was that,' Anne-Marie is reported as saying. From then onwards the young Greek prince was a regular visitor to Copenhagen and frequently escorted all three of the Danish princesses, though most people thought he was quietly courting Princess Benedikte, Anne-Marie's attractive elder sister.

The following summer, when she was fifteen, Anne-Marie went to Norway for a holiday with her former governess. Constantine, a skilled sailor, was there at the same time to enter his yacht in a series of races. They saw quite a lot of each other. There was no doubt now that they were falling in love. The Prince decided impetuously that he must make sure Anne-Marie knew how he felt. He asked her to marry him when she was old enough. She was over the moon with joy, for she knew there would never be anyone else as far as she was concerned. She had been in love with him from the moment she saw him. So far it was almost like a Hans Andersen fairy story, but they still had to face reality, and their parents.

When King Frederick was told, the normally affable monarch exploded. What were they thinking of? His daughter was still at school! She was still too young, far too young, to even *think* of getting engaged. Anne-Marie wept and pleaded with her father until his heart softened. He could see that the young couple really were meant for each other. But he was adamant on one point. Anne-Marie could not marry until she had finished her education at eighteen. They could not become engaged until she was sixteen and no announcement of any kind would be made until then. He swore the couple to secrecy and insisted that Prince Constantine went back home to Greece until the time came.

Anne-Marie's friends guessed that something was going on though she kept her promise to her father and never gave away her secret. They noticed, however, that she was always rushing back to the palace early when they went out for the evening, because she was expecting a phone call from Greece. While they were apart Constantine and Anne-Marie talked to each other almost every night.

When Princess Anne-Marie was sixteen King Frederick kept his promise. In January 1963 he announced to the world that his lovely young daughter was engaged to the prince who would one day be King of the Hellenes. The princess, who had had to be silent about her love for so long, now talked of nothing but Constantine, how handsome he was, what wonderful brown eyes he had. The Prince, equally in love, counted the moments until he could see her. On her seventeenth birthday he impetuously flew to Denmark to surprise her with a serenade of 'Happy Birthday to You' and armfuls of flowers.

The wedding was fixed for 18 September 1964, when Anne-Marie would be eighteen. News of the match was received with great pleasure in Greece as there had always been accord between the two royal houses. The history of the Greek throne had been turbulent enough in the past and though King Paul, Constantine's father, a fine, good man, was regarded with affection, there were mixed feelings about Queen Frederika, who had made herself unpopular by meddling too much in politics. The Greeks now looked at Constantine with intense interest as he was to be their future king.

Constantine was born at Psychico, a villa belonging to his parents near Athens, on 2 June 1940. His father was then Crown Prince. His mother, the dynamically attractive and controversial Frederika, was the only daughter of the Duke of Brunswick, head of the royal house of Hanover, and great-great-grand-daughter of Queen Victoria.

His childhood was dramatically affected by the war years. When the Germans invaded Greece the royal family were hustled out of Athens in an R.A.F. Sunderland flying boat and landed in Crete. When bombs started raining on Crete they fled to Egypt, and eventually settled in South Africa. Constantine had twenty different homes in five years but because the family relationships were strong and affectionate it did not seem to affect him. Field Marshal Jan Smuts, the South African Prime Minister, was like a father to the young Tino and his sister Sophia.

When they returned to Greece after the war there was the Communist threat, desperate poverty among the peasants and much bitterness. Constantine grew up in a Greece rent by riot and turbulence. After initial teaching at home he attended a school founded by his parents on progressive, democratic lines. He then went to military training and attended lectures at Athens University but, as students were only too often mixed up in political riots and strikes, it soon became impossible for him to continue. It was not thought advisable for the Crown Prince to be connected with such controversial activity. He quietly carried on his studies in constitutional law, economics and military history under private tutors. His mother insisted that he took a course in fundamental nuclear physics to equip him for the nuclear age.

With his sisters Sophia and Irene Tino, as he was always called in the family, enjoyed a happy, robust family life. There was a special bond between the Prince and his father. Both had a deep love of the sea. Both were passionately devoted to Greece. Ever since he was ten years old, whenever his lessons allowed it, Tino attended all his father's audiences and conferences, sitting quietly in a corner, listening and learning. Only when he came of age at eighteen was he asked his opinion. Constantine grew up to be enterprising and independent, but because father and son thought and acted in a similar way on matters of importance, the Prince gradually became his father's trusted aide.

Queen Frederika, in her autobiography, describes the day when Constantine came of age and had to take his oath to the King as an officer of the Greek armed forces. 'Everybody was in full dress uniform or evening clothes. The government armed forces were all lined up around the reception room in the old Athens palace while Tino, in a slow and steady voice, took his oath. Father and son never looked at each other. They knew if they did the emotion would be too strong and impossible to control. They were both immensely proud of each other. It was a pride that had its roots in deep mutual love and devotion.' Soon after the ceremony his parents left for a visit abroad and for the first time, at the tender age of eighteen, Constantine had to take on the full responsibility as regent. He acquitted himself well.

The Prince was a splendid sportsman, a strong swimmer, a third-degree karate black belt, a vigorous squash player – but above all a fine yachtsman. King Paul was a born sailor and handled a boat as well as any naval officer, but he had to hand the laurels to his son in the summer of 1960. Constantine, now twenty years old, had made up his mind to compete in the Olympics. For months he got up at five o'clock in the morning so that he could practise in his boat before settling down to his studies. The yacht had been given to him by the Royal Greek Navy as a coming-of-age present and he felt he ought to use it to bring glory home to Greece.

In 1960 the Olympic Games were held in Italy. He led the Greek team into the stadium at the opening ceremony and went on to win a gold medal. After his moment of triumph his overjoyed family greeted him with a boisterous display of affection coupled with a reminder not to let the victory go to his head. His sister Sophia turned a hosepipe on him, and his father threw him back into the sea and let him swim ashore!

In February 1964 King Paul became seriously ill with cancer and Constantine suddenly found himself regent again. On 6 March, two weeks after an operation, the sailor King died and Crown Prince Constantine succeeded him. He took his formal oath a week later.

Though deeply grieved by his father's death, the young King had his marriage to Anne-Marie to look forward to. Already popular, Constantine, at the age of twenty-four, was bringing home a bride of whom the Greek people could approve. They could also see that, in a sphere in which many marriages are still arranged by diplomats, this royal match was a genuine love story. The eighteen-year-old Princess and the King were seen walking together hand-in-hand and were once even spotted in the back of a royal limousine with their arms around each other. Anne-Marie had given up all her claims to the Danish throne for this marriage. She had also given up her Protestant faith as a member of the Evangelical Lutheran Church to become Greek Orthodox like her husband.

There were rumblings of political trouble, of course, but they were momentarily forgotten on the September day in 1964 when King Constantine II of the Hellenes married Princess Anne-Marie of Denmark in a ceremony both romantic and spectacular. The wedding took place in the Byzantine splendour of the Metropolis, the Greek Orthodox Cathedral in Athens. A million people lined the streets of the city to watch the procession. Thousands camped out on the pavements overnight.

The young King, resplendent in full field marshal's uniform, complete with baton, drove through the crowded streets in an open carriage with his mother by his side. There followed an open landau drawn by six greys carrying the King of Denmark and his lovely daughter, about to become Queen of Greece. She was a fairy-tale princess, slender, vulnerably young, dressed in a high-waisted gown of white satin with a veil of lace held off her face with a diamond tiara. Rather touchingly, she carried a simple bouquet of lilies-of-the-valley sent from the royal castle gardens in Denmark. Her twenty-foot train was carried by six royal princesses, among them England's Princess Anne, all gowned in white organza.

Inside the cathedral were seven reigning monarchs with their consorts, two reigning princes, two ex-kings, two queen mothers and over a hundred princes and princesses. Prince Philip, Constantine's second cousin, was there with his mother, who was wearing the simple grey habit of the Greek Orthodox order to which she belonged.

Silver icons gleamed on the ancient walls and sprays and garlands of red gladioli were in profusion everywhere. When Anne-Marie reached Constantine's side she bowed slightly and smiled. He returned the smile warmly and bent to kiss her hand tenderly. An almost audible sigh rippled through the congregation. The Primate of Greece, Archbishop Chrysostomos, wearing his gold episcopal crown and glittering robes, began reciting the words of the ceremony as a one-hundred-and-one-gun salute boomed across the city. Throughout the ceremony the two young people constantly spoke to each other in murmurs and looked into each other's eyes. The aged Metropolitan took the gold wedding rings and the ritual, symbolizing the mystic union of the Holy Trinity, began. Three times the wedding rings, one for the bridegroom, one for the bride, were slipped on to their fingers. Three times the King and his bride were crowned with the gilt marriage crowns and three times they sipped wine from the communion chalice.

When it was all over the eighteen-year-old Queen was seen to be trying hard to hold back the tears of joy that streamed down her face as she stood before the altar holding the King's arm.

As they drove back to the palace through cheering crowds, rose petals showered into their open landau, guns boomed in salute and church bells pealed out over the ancient, sun-baked city. People cheered themselves hoarse and threw streamers in the national colours of both Greece and Denmark. Everyone felt that the young Queen had brought with her hopes of a happy and successful reign. The correspondent for the London *Times*, in Athens for the wedding, said, 'The newlyweds conquered the hearts of the sentimental Greeks by their youth, their good looks and their evident love for each other.'

After a wedding breakfast for eighty at the palace the King and Queen left in their private aircraft for a honeymoon on one of the Greek islands. Before they departed Anne-Marie touched the hearts of both her new husband and her mother-in-law, Queen Frederika, by asking for her wedding bouquet to be placed on the grave of King Paul.

Anne-Marie had not, she admitted later, expected to become Queen quite so soon. But for the tragic death of King Paul she and her young husband would have had time in which to enjoy life together before taking on their immense responsibilities. As it was, they were thrown in at the deep end together. Anne-Marie had virtually stepped straight from the schoolroom into her new role as Queen. She had very little experience of the outside world. First she had to learn about politics, a potent, ever-erupting force in Greece. She took lessons in modern Greek, not an easy language to learn. One of her greatest allies was the formidable Queen Frederika, who, she said, had been wonderful to her. Bravely, the young Danish girl added, 'I feel that I must be entirely Greek. I don't mean that one should forget the country where one was born, but my mother, who was Swedish, told me that when she married she immediately and consciously became part of Denmark.'

Constantine and Anne-Marie enjoyed a honeymoon period of about eighteen months. They had inherited an enormous fund of goodwill from the reign of King Paul and for a time the normal turbulence associated with Greek politics seemed to be stilled. The whole of Greece could see that the King and Queen were in love. They walked about hand-in-hand. When she mentioned him to others her eyes softened and she could not help but sing his praises. They spent as much time as possible together. She loved to watch him play squash and often joined him on the tennis court, though he always beat her. She went sailing with him, but only as a passenger, protesting that she had not enough confidence to crew. Sometimes they would go dancing together, but on the whole they preferred to be at home in the evenings when there were no official functions.

Besides taking on the job of Queen long before she had expected to, Anne-Marie also had to learn how to control and organize the every-day life of the royal household – not, one would have thought, an easy task for an eighteen-year-old. She was thankful to find an already smooth-running régime but pointed out with youthful, touching pride when interviewed by *The Times*, 'I keep an eye on the work everybody has to do – and I know whether they are doing it properly or not.' The young Queen had a Swiss housekeeper and after her first baby arrived an English nanny, but there was also a Greek nanny and most of the household staff were Greek.

King Constantine, she revealed, enjoyed good food. 'I choose it for him. The cook sends up a choice of menus but sometimes I select something completely different.' She added, 'We make a point of having all our meals together. Whatever time my husband comes in – or however late – I always wait for him.' Sometimes they would slip out to a restaurant for lunch or dinner. They preferred to go alone, just like any other young married couple.

If they felt like something grand they would order a table at one of the sophisticated international hotels in Athens but often they would pop into one of the small tavernas in the old quarter of Athens under the walls of the Acropolis.

When she lived at home in Denmark Anne-Marie often used to go shopping without attracting much attention but she found it was not possible to stroll casually in the streets of Athens without drawing a large, enthusiastic crowd. Sometimes in the evenings she and the King would quietly leave by the side gate of the palace and walk hand-in-hand down the quiet streets nearby. At Tatoi, the country estate where they preferred to spend most of their time, they were much freer to take walks when they pleased, even pushing Crown Princess Alexia in her pram.

Constantine put a great deal of his faith in the royal motto 'My strength lies in the love of my people,' and for the first period of his reign the faith proved justified. But he also knew that since Otto of Bavaria was called to the Greek throne in 1829, after Greece had been liberated from four hundred years of Turkish domination, not a single king had reigned for his full term. George I was assassinated; Constantine I abdicated twice; George II left the country and was restored twice; the unfortunate Alexander I died as the result of a bite from one of his pet monkeys. Even King Paul's reign had been cut short by his untimely death.

He must, then, have felt some trepidation when the rumblings of discontent began to escalate into violence in the third year of his reign. The births of their daughter Alexia and their son Crown Prince Paul had given Constantine and Anne-Marie great joy. But soon news of the riots and demonstrations in favour of a new form of government and against the monarchy could not be ignored, even though they were somewhat isolated from them in the Tatoi Royal Palace where they lived surrounded by 11,000 acres of land, sixteen miles outside Athens.

Soon it became clear that Greece was to experience another enormous political upheaval. The crisis came in 1967. A junta composed of the infamous Greek colonels seized power and swiftly established a military dictatorship. Though many people were still royalist and supported Constantine, it was obvious that the Crown was in danger and that the young King's reign was hanging by a thread.

In December 1967, eight months after the colonels had taken over, Constantine bravely attempted a counter coup – but the attempt went badly wrong. Army tanks surrounded the palace and the King and Queen had no other choice but to remove themselves and their children from danger and fly into exile.

King Constantine's reign had only lasted for three years and nine months but he still had Anne-Marie at his side. They flew from a secret airport in pouring rain, a tragic contrast to the shining, confident figures on that memorable wedding day. When he took his seat on the plane, grim and silent, he put his arm comfortingly around his wife. She was pregnant.

They arrived at Rome airport in the pre-dawn darkness. Constantine stepped down from the plane holding his little daughter, Alexia, by the hand. He was in uniform but had shrugged on a duffel-type overcoat and looked haggard. A nurse followed carrying the baby Prince Paul. Anne-Marie, wrapped in a fur coat, shivered in the cold. Their luggage seemed to consist of nine small suitcases.

At first they took refuge in the Greek Embassy but violent left-wing demonstrations eventually drove them to take cover in a private villa belonging to Prince Heinrich of Hesse. Not long afterwards, Anne-Marie was rushed to a clinic where she lost her baby. The strain had been too much. The King remained by her side, sleeping on a divan in her room at the clinic. When they left she was seen to be weeping, supported by the twenty-seven-year-old ex-King, who was distraught.

When they had recovered slightly from the profound shock of losing first their country, then their baby, Constantine and Anne-Marie decided to settle in England where they had many friends in the British royal family. Their first home in exile was at Chobham in Surrey but they finally settled in a handsome, ten-bedroomed house standing in five acres of land in Hampstead Garden Suburb on the outskirts of London. They have lived there ever since in a luxurious but hardly royal setting. They left behind them the palace at Tatoi filled with ancient Greek pottery and priceless Byzantine art treasures as well as their summer palace, Mon Repos, in Corfu. But it is said that Queen Anne-Marie did not leave behind the so-called Romanov jewels but that she managed to bring them with her when they fled. They are an heirloom, passed on from one Queen of Greece to the next, consisting of a tiara and brooch of emeralds said to be worth in the region of two million pounds.

Constantine and Anne-Marie have only been back to Greece once since that traumatic night when they went into exile. It was a sad occasion: the funeral of Queen Frederika, who died of a heart attack when she was sixty-three in February 1981.

It was the first time Constantine had set foot on Greek soil for thirteen years. As he stepped from the plane he fell to his knees and kissed the ground, making the sign of the cross. The Athens government made a determined effort to prevent the public from seeing the ex-King, knowing there were factions that still supported the monarchy. But a thousand supporters surged around them, tried to lift Constantine shoulder high and shouted, 'Stay here for ever.' The ex-King tried to calm them in spite of his own overwhelming emotion.

They could not stay at Tatoi, the palace which remained his personal property, because it was so run down and instead they had to put up at a small hotel nearby. They were in Greece for six hours and had to leave immediately after the funeral.

Favourites with the British royals, Constantine and Anne-Marie have carved out a new life for themselves in England. They now have five children. Prince Nicholas was born after they went into exile and another happy event took place on 20 October 1983 when, after several miscarriages, their fourth child, Princess Theodora, was christened at the Greek Orthodox Cathedral in London. It was an occasion for the most extraordinary gathering of European royalty and for a while Moscow Road, Bayswater, was jammed with diplomatic cars and others flying royal pennants. King Constantine had arrived an hour before the ceremony carrying a container of holy water from the River Jordan which was to be used for the christening. As he climbed the Cathedral steps a few old Greek women who had been waiting for hours called out to him, 'We pray for you.' Four-months-old Princess Theodora, stripped naked for the actual christening according to Orthodox ritual, began to cry lustily until one of her godmothers, our own Queen Elizabeth, leaned across and gently cradled her head. Immediately the crying stopped. Some saw it as a good omen for the future. Their eldest son, Crown Prince Paul, is at Sandhurst and their youngest, Prince Philippos, was born at St Mary's Hospital, Paddington in April 1986 and christened at the Greek Orthodox Cathedral, where the ceremony was attended by two kings, three queens, twenty-five princes, and the Princess of Wales was one of the seven godparents. Constantine himself is godfather to Prince William, son of the Prince and Princess of Wales.

Though the monarchy has been abolished officially in Greece and a republic established following a popular referendum, the ex-King still refuses to relinquish his claim to the throne and lives in the hope that one day he will be able to return from exile. But in all his troubles he has had the support of a wife who has adored him since she was twelve years old and whose devotion has been evident in the very difficult times they have endured together.

# Princess Margaret
## —AND—
# Peter Townsend

The Coronation of Queen Elizabeth II was over. In the Annexe of Westminster Abbey, waiting for their carriages, kings and queens mingled with nobility, politicians and commoners. The atmosphere was electric, for the historic ritual had moved and thrilled everyone there. No one was more elated than the Queen's sister, Princess Margaret, exquisite in her ceremonial robes and coronet. She was talking excitedly to a slender, handsome young man in the uniform of a high-ranking R.A.F. officer. Their eyes met and, oblivious to the crowds around her, she reached up and brushed a piece of fluff off his shoulder. There was something fond and intimate about the gesture. It did not go unobserved. In that one unguarded moment on 2 June 1953 Princess Margaret revealed to the world that she was in love with a royal equerry, Group Captain Peter Townsend, war hero, favourite of the royal family – but a divorced man with two sons.

For several years before her sister ascended the throne, twenty-three-year-old Princess Margaret had lived a sparkling social life, trailing after her an adoring and admiring string of aristocratic young men including the Lords Porchester and Blandford, the Earl of Dalkeith, Billy Wallace and Dominic Elliot. Many thought that while Elizabeth had found complete fulfilment in her happy marriage to Prince Philip and her role as heir to the throne, Princess Margaret felt left out, always second in line. She solved the problem by creating her own circle, 'The Margaret Set', and leading a glamorous social life. She loved parties, theatres, smart restaurants and nightclubs. Gossip columns sizzled with Margaret stories as she danced the foxtrot and samba with verve, stayed out as late as she liked, smoked cigarettes in an ivory holder, drank champagne and devasted her captive admirers with scintillating humour and wit.

Everyone thought that she would eventually choose a husband from the group of wealthy, elegant young men who, along with two or three close girl friends, made up 'The Set'. Nobody guessed that from the age of fourteen Princess Margaret had had a 'crush' on the Battle of Britain hero who became her father's aide, or that that teenage emotion would one day turn into a passionate love that would threaten chaos in the royal family and bring the weight of the Establishment and Church down on her pretty head.

Perhaps she was ill-starred, as far as love is concerned, from the beginning. More recent years have seen her married and divorced, involved with a younger man considered 'unsuitable', in need of a satisfactory relationship for her more mature years. But it was the fact that she was forced to deny her love for Peter Townsend that makes her one of the royal family's most romantic figures and the Margaret–Townsend affair one of the great love stories of our time.

When Princess Margaret was born at Glamis Castle on the night of 21 August 1930, the second child of King George VI, then still Duke of York, and the former Lady Elizabeth Bowes Lyon, his Duchess, there was a terrific thunderstorm and wild rejoicings. Glamis, the ancestral home of the Strathmores, Lady Elizabeth's family, lies twelve miles north of Dundee. This was the first royal birth of any significance north of the border for more than three centuries. It had been the Duchess of York's decision to have her second child at Glamis, her family's seat since 1372, as a tribute to Scotland and her ancestry. The baby was christened Margaret Rose at Buckingham Palace in the royal family's gold, lily-shaped font containing water from the river Jordan and declared to be a beautiful child.

While her sister Lilibet, four years older and one day to be Queen Elizabeth II, always showed a certain seriousness and sense of responsibility, Princess Margaret was mercurial, a lively, enchanting toddler who, it was said, could actually hum the waltz from *The Merry Widow* at the age of nine months. From the beginning Lilibet was protective, always ready to defend her amusing, naughty little sister. Those close to the family said that while Princess Elizabeth was the Duke of York's pride, Margaret was his joy. She could wheedle him out of his dark moods, clambering on his knee and making him laugh with her quick childish chatter.

The most traumatic experience of her childhood was the abdication of Edward VIII when Lilibet told her 'Uncle David is going away and isn't coming back and papa is to be King.' The wide-eyed six-year-old asked, 'Does that mean one day you are going to be Queen?' When also told that she could no longer sign herself as Margaret Rose of York she cried, 'But that means I'm nothing!' These were first indications of a problem many feel she has suffered from all her life: trying to find her rightful place in the scheme of things and experiencing the difficulty of being number two.

She was not yet seven when her parents were crowned in Westminster Abbey. The sisters were dressed alike in white lace trimmed with silver bows. Each wore a lightweight coronet made to the King's special order and trains of purple velvet trimmed with ermine. Margaret kicked up a fuss because Lilibet's train was longer than hers. For the young princess the worst part of papa becoming King was the fact that the family had to move from their comfortable home at 145 Piccadilly to live in Buckingham Palace where her cries of, 'Lilibet, wait for me, wait for me!' echoed down the endless corridors.

By the time she was ten years old Princess Margaret was a character to be reckoned with. She was a clever mimic, her tongue was witty beyond her years and she was full of mischief. Even Queen Mary, her regally austere grandmother, said, 'The child is so outrageously amusing that one can't help encouraging her.' Some of her high spirits were let off through theatrical performances which were just as popular with Princess Elizabeth. She loved dressing up in a crinoline and powdered wig to play Cinderella to Lilibet's Prince Charming and brought a tear to the King's eye when, angelically dressed all in white, she sang 'Gentle Jesus, Meek and Mild' in a Christmas nativity play.

When the Second World War broke out George VI refused to leave London but kept his daughters at Balmoral out of harm's way. They were reunited with their parents at Sandringham in February 1940, three months later being transferred to a sand-bagged, blacked-out Windsor Castle where they stayed until hostilities ceased. They were kept to a strict routine and their lessons were not allowed to be interrupted. 'Poor dears, they haven't had much fun,' said the King at the end of the war.

As they grew older Margaret began to realize more clearly than ever that while her sister's role was definite, hers was not. Elizabeth became involved with more and more things that did not concern her younger sister. She became her father's shadow, had access to the mysterious red boxes containing State papers and took lessons in constitutional history from Sir Henry Marten, Vice Provost of Eton. Even more impressive to teenage Margaret was the arrival on the scene of handsome, fair-haired Prince Philip of Greece, a dashing bronzed naval officer who spent his Christmas leave with the royal family at Windsor in 1944 and succumbed almost immediately to the lovely smile and quiet charm of Princess Elizabeth. Margaret noticed that Lilibet began to take more and more care with her makeup and hair, more interest in her clothes. Whenever Prince Philip was around she positively glowed.

When Princess Margaret was fourteen and watching her sister fall in love her father made a fateful decision. He had a great desire to honour the brave young men who had fought for Britain so, when he needed a new equerry, instead of looking among established courtiers he asked Air Chief Marshal Sir Charles Portal, Chief of Air Staff, to send him someone with 'a good fighting record'.

So it was that on 16 February 1944 Group Captain Peter Townsend found himself standing to attention in the green-carpeted Regency room at Buckingham Palace while the King eyed him keenly. Townsend was a handsome young man, elegant, slender in his R.A.F. uniform. His record showed that he was a fighter pilot of extraordinary courage. He had been born in Burma where his father was commissioner of the Pegu division and a member of the Legislative Council – one of the handful of Englishmen who at that time ruled fifteen million Burmese. Peter Townsend spent only his earliest years there but throughout his life he has had a special love for Burma and its people. His father retired in 1917 and brought his family back to England, settling in the West Country where his ancestors, all Devon men, had lived for centuries. Peter grew up in rambling houses at Tavistock and Bideford with the thunder of the Atlantic on the north Devon rocks never far away. His childhood was happy in a close-knit family but he was sent away to Haileybury School to be educated, a place where he felt the most important lesson he learned in five tough years was survival.

When he was thirteen a marvellous thing happened. He discovered flying. His housemaster, Mr Ashcroft, an understanding man, arranged one day for him to be taken up from the R.A.F. base at Old Sarum, near Salisbury. He had to present his father's written permission for the venture and sign a 'blood chit', absolving the R.A.F. from responsibility in case of an accident. Tucked into the back cockpit of a Bristol Fighter, a World War One biplane, he watched the grass and the golden fields of corn slipping away below until the plane reached a height at which they seemed to be poised, motionless. 'Looking out along the wings I could not believe that we were flying through the air were it not for the slipstream pressing like a cold, strong hand against my face, exhilarating me and taking my breath away. That flight decided me. I would become a pilot,' he wrote in his memoirs *Time and Chance*.

He became a cadet at Cranwell, the R.A.F. College in Lincolnshire, made his fist solo flight in 1933 when he was eighteen and two years later joined the crack No 1 Fighter Squadron at Tangmere in Sussex. He was in his element.

With the outbreak of war Peter Townsend became one of the brilliant young fighter pilots who helped to defend Britain's coastal approaches. In February 1940 the squadron he led shot down the first enemy bomber over English soil. Stepping into the cockpit of a Spitfire he then joined 'The Few' who defended London in the Battle of Britain. Day after day he led his squadron against the German Luftwaffe until he was injured in the foot. He returned to fly Hurricanes against the Germans until twenty months of day and night operations took their toll. 'The fight had gone out of me,' he wrote. 'I was flying more like a tired chicken than an avenging angel.' R.A.F. doctors grounded him and for the rest of the war he commanded mostly from fighter stations, only briefly making a comeback as commander of 605 Night Fighter Squadron. He had married a tall, lovely English girl called Rosemary, daughter of Sir Timothy Pawle of Hundson in Hertfordshire. It was a typical wartime marriage, happiness snatched at the height of battle destined to dwindle and fade.

Group Captain Townsend, then, had about him all the charisma of a fighter ace. His interview with the King went well. As he left the Regency room he met Sir Piers Legh, Master of the Household, and paused to thank him for the briefing he had given him before his meeting with the King. 'Down the corridor,' he wrote, 'came two adorable-looking girls, all smiles, Princess Elizabeth and Princess Margaret. Our meeting might have been a coincidence, but, thinking back, I would not have put it beyond the King to have buzzed them on the interphone and told them, "If you want to see him, he's just leaving my study." Elizabeth, then seventeeen, and Margaret, fourteen, spent most of their time leading a sequestered life at Windsor Castle and the faintest curiosity like myself could brighten it.'

Two weeks later Peter Townsend took up his duties as equerry. He found himself absorbed into the royal family and treated so thoughtfully he felt more like a guest than an aide. As a member of the 'Household in Waiting' he shared not only the King's hours on duty but also his time of relaxation, lunching and dining with the family, walking, riding and shooting with them as well. Sometimes the irrepressible Princess Margaret would urge him to take part in bicycle races round and round the gravelled paths at Windsor or to play her at Canasta, a game at which she usually triumphed. He thought her a delightful and amusing teenager. She regarded him with something akin to hero worship.

Originally it was intended that Townsend should stay with the King for three months but his appointment was such a success it was decided to keep him as a permanent equerry. He was eventually given a 'grace and favour' house, Adelaide Cottage, in the Home Park of Windsor Castle and when not on duty lived there with his wife and two sons. His life as an equerry meant that he came into contact with kings, queens, emperors, foreign dignitaries as a matter of routine, and travelled extensively. While he tried to keep his feet on the ground, it was a heady experience and began to affect his marriage.

In the winter of 1946 he learned that he would be required to accompany the King, the Queen and the two princesses on a tour of South Africa and Rhodesia. The visit, in response to a long-standing invitation from Field Marshal Smuts, was considered an important one. They would be leaving England on 1 February 1947 and would be away for three months. Townsend, still deeply attached to his wife and aware that he was to some extent neglecting her by leaving her alone for so long with their two small sons, nevertheless felt excited at the prospect. He had an adventurous spirit and was thirsty for new experiences and his first sight of Africa, a continent he had never seen. Princess Margaret, now sixteen and taking on the bloom of a beautiful young woman, was bursting with excitement about the trip. She was by now deep in the throes of a teenage infatuation for a man twice her age. All that mattered was that for three whole months he would be in Africa with them, always somewhere in the background. Poor Elizabeth was the only one who didn't want to go. Deeply in love with Prince Philip, she could not bear the thought of being parted from him for so long and was well aware that the separation was deliberate, regarded by her parents as a test of their feelings for each other.

Under the glorious South African sun Princess Margaret slowly came into the full flower of her young womanhood. She basked in the admiration showered upon her. At the beginning of the tour, in Cape Town, she appeared at a ceremonial ball in her first really grand evening dress made from sixty yards of tulle and was hailed as Britain's Dresden china princess.

From Cape Town the royal family, with an entourage that included Townsend, set off on a two months' marathon to meet the people of South Africa and Rhodesia. They travelled most of the way in a magnificently appointed, fully air conditioned white train, but stopped hundreds of times to greet people of all races who responded warmly to the simplicity and sincerity of the King and Queen. Sometimes at dawn Townsend would take the two princesses for a gallop along the white beaches of the coastal plain or, inland, across the veldt, just as it was awakening at sunrise. These excursions were remembered long after some of the more formal moments had faded from their memories. Townsend wrote home to his wife, 'You must come with me one day to this lovely place.'

Photographs of Princess Margaret taken in South Africa, with Peter Townsend hovering in the background, seem to show a certain awareness of each other, captured by the camera but only meaningful in retrospect.

Back home in England all attention was on Princess Elizabeth, radiant with happiness when her engagement to Prince Philip was finally announced on 10 July 1947. For the rest of that year the royal family were absorbed in preparations for the wedding in November and Margaret, as chief bridesmaid, joined fully in the excitement, stifling the sadness she could not help but feel at the thought of losing her sister and closest companion. She had to get to know her future brother-in-law, newly created Duke of Edinburgh by the King. There were rehearsals at Westminster Abbey. There were also endless dress fittings at which royal couturier Norman Hartnell, like a magician, produced yards and yards of rich, stiff satin, silk and lace, thousands of pearls to be sewn on the bridal gown, all to make a wedding that would break the post-war austerity and raise everyone's spirits.

At the glittering ball held at Buckingham Palace the night before the wedding, Princess Elizabeth, wearing the magnificent diamond necklace given to her on her twenty-first birthday in South Africa, was naturally the focus of attention. She had never looked prettier. But Princess Margaret, moving gracefully among the young royals from foreign countries, was obviously just as fascinating to most people present. She would surely be next to marry. Who would she choose? Was there anyone special? Margaret, in sparkling form, gave nothing away.

As she had anticipated, she missed Lilibet terribly and it was decided she should start her public duties on a full-time basis as soon as possible to give her a purpose in life. She celebrated her eighteenth birthday in the late summer of 1948 and a few weeks later represented the King at Queen Juliana's inauguration on a four-day visit to The Netherlands. Wearing an elegant full-length, rose-pink dress with a matching ostrich feather hat she attracted considerable attention. She was now a beautiful young woman with great poise. Peter Townsend, included in Margaret's entourage on this occasion, admitted later, 'Without realizing it, I was being carried a little further from home, a little nearer the Princess.'

Over the next three years Princess Margaret fulfilled all her royal duties conscientiously. At night however she turned into a social butterfly. She led 'The Set' with her closest girl friends, who included the gregarious Sharman Douglas, blonde daughter of the American Ambassador in London, or Lady Caroline Montagu Douglas Scott, niece of the Duchess of Gloucester. As they watched her flit from nightclub to nightclub some people felt that her behaviour was uncomfortably like that of her Uncle David, who in his heyday as the glamorous Prince of Wales dominated London's social scene.

She would make her grand entrance into one exclusive night spot or another with a galaxy of elegant young aristocrats in attendance. Wearing fashionable, strapless evening dresses, her cornflower-blue eyes sparkling, she flaunted royal convention by smoking in public. With an ivory cigarette holder in one hand and champagne glass in the other she held court. But she never forgot she was royal. If anyone overstepped the mark her eyes would become ice-cold and distant.

The first of the young aristocrats to be mentioned as a possible husband was the Duke of Buccleuch's heir, the Earl of Dalkeith, a tall, fair-haired war-time naval officer. But they just remained good friends. Other famous members of the 'Margaret Set' were 'Sonny' Blandford, the Duke of Marlborough's heir, Simon Ward, son of the Earl of Dudley, and Billy Wallace, tall, gangling, elegant, with beautiful manners and a keen sense of humour. But one by one they married other girls and Margaret took into her 'Set' men who reflected the more serious side of her nature – the Rev. Simon Phipps, with whom she discussed religion, and Mark Bonham Carter, who could appreciate her love of Keats, Chaucer and Shakespeare. Then there was always her long-standing, faithful friend Colin Tennant, heir to Lord Glenconner, who stood by her in difficult days ahead.

While she basked in the admiration of these elegant, wealthy young men and danced with them until the early hours of the morning, few guessed that she was struggling to understand her own feelings for Peter Townsend.

In the autumn of 1951 the royal family were at Balmoral as usual. The King had been advised to stay in the Highlands as long as possible for a much-needed rest. His health was beginning to cause some concern. Princess Margaret and a small group of household staff including Group Captain Townsend, now assistant Master of the Household, were with the King and Queen. The weather was idyllic with blue skies and cool, clear air. One day after a picnic lunch with the guns, Townsend stretched out on the heather to doze. 'Then, vaguely, I was aware that someone was covering me with a coat,' he wrote in *Time and Chance*. 'I opened one eye to see Princess Margaret's lovely face, very close, looking into mine. Then I opened the other eye and saw, behind her, the King, leaning on his stick with a certain look, typical of him: kind, half amused. I whispered, "You know your father is watching us?" at which she laughed, straightened up and went to his side. Then, she took his arm and walked him away, leaving me to my dreams.'

On another occasion the King had run into the pair of them on the stairs. Townsend was carrying Margaret and they were laughing, her arms wrapped around his neck. The King looked angry until Margaret, who always knew how to placate her father, cried out, 'Don't be cross, Papa, I asked him to! I *ordered* him!' Whether the King took it all as a demonstration of youthful high spirits or whether, with his sensitive nature, he guessed what was happening and feared for his daughter's happiness, we shall never know.

Their feelings were not out in the open yet. In fact it was to be another twelve months before Townsend dared to admit to himself what he really felt for the King's daughter and some time after that before he declared his love. Princess Margaret, fortified by all the instincts and training of a member of the royal family, kept up a vivacious façade. She took on a heavier work-load, travelled abroad, where in Italy and France she was given film-star treatment by the press, celebrated her twenty-first birthday in style and constantly set off fresh rumours about whom she favoured as a future bridegroom. She had only to dance twice with someone for speculations to begin. Only the Queen and the Queen Mother knew something of her dilemma.

The death of King George VI at Sandringham on 5 February 1952 came as a heavy blow to the whole royal family. Though he was only fifty-six years old, he had slowly succumbed to the stress and strain of being thrust upon the throne without preparation and leading his country through the terrible years of war. His doctors diagnosed lung cancer. Princess Margaret, who adored her father, found it hard to come to terms with what had happened and was at first inconsolable. Her mother was trying to cope with her own deep grief; her sister was taken further away from her by the mystery of monarchy and the fact that she was now Queen. She found spiritual help in her religious beliefs, which were deep rooted. For more earthly comfort she turned increasingly to the man who had been in the background of her life for so many years, her father's own equerry, whom he had treated as a son.

Ten months after the King's death a brief notice in the press announced that Group Captain Peter Woolridge Townsend had been granted a decree nisi in the divorce court on the grounds of misconduct by his wife, Cecil Rosemary, with Mr John de Laszlo, an export merchant. There was no doubt that Peter's prolonged absences during the eight years he had served as equerry had put an intolerable strain on a marriage that had been foundering for some time.

By the end of 1952 it was obvious that things had changed drastically as far as Margaret and Townsend were concerned. The Princess was now of age; Townsend was free. The latter had assumed even greater responsibility. At the request of the Queen Mother he accepted the office of Comptroller to her Household. Princess Margaret moved from Buckingham Palace to live with her mother at Clarence House, so the two were under the same roof again. Townsend had offered Margaret a shoulder to lean on while he himself had been under great strain through the break-up of his marriage. Now they seemed to be together every moment he was off duty. He even helped her choose the colour scheme for her private suite.

Though talk was beginning to circulate at a low voltage among the courtiers and servants at Clarence House, Buckingham Palace and Windsor, nothing was passed on to the outside world. One afternoon early in 1953 the couple were alone together at Windsor Castle. Everyone had gone to London for some ceremony or other. They sat for hours in front of the fire in the Red Drawing-room and for the first time the talk was entirely about themselves. When Peter Townsend finally confessed his love for her, Princess Margaret answered, 'That's how I feel, too.'

They were not able to meet openly but their clandestine meetings increased until they were spending most of their free time together. One afternoon Townsend took Margaret to his sister's house for tea; they would slip away to the cinema together, seek solitude in early-morning rides and take refuge in the apartments of sympathetic and understanding friends who had been let into the secret.

Even years later, writing in his memoirs, Townsend is obviously overwhelmed by the memory of her: 'She was a girl of unusual, intense beauty ... large, purple-blue eyes, generous, sensitive lips and a complexion as smooth as a peach. She was capable in her face and in her whole being of an astonishing power of expression. She was by nature generous, volatile. She was a comedienne at heart, coquettish, sophisticated.' But, he said, what ultimately made her so attractive and lovable was that behind the dazzling façade, the apparant self-assurance, you found if you looked for it, a rare softness and sincerity. 'She could make you bend double with laughing, she could also touch you deeply.'

However hard they tried to be circumspect the fact that they were in love was now obvious to those in close contact with them. Palace diehards began to talk of 'Scandal' and 'Threat to the Monarchy'. As there was no longer any question of hiding their love from those nearest to them, they decided to tell the Queen and the Queen Mother that they loved each other and would like to marry. Elizabeth, while sympathetic and only too aware that Margaret longed for the same sort of happiness that she had found with Prince Philip, had no illusions about the difficult times ahead. Townsend was, after all, divorced. The Queen Mother, still grieving for the King, longed for her husband's wise counsels. She knew George VI had loved Peter Townsend like a son and would have known exactly what to do. His divorce threw up shades of the Prince of Wales and Mrs Simpson and made her shudder.

The Queen asked to see Princess Margaret and Peter Townsend together so that they could talk things over. She made it clear that she had no personal directive but asked them if they would wait for a year. Her sister's wish to marry a divorcé, even if he was the innocent party, placed the Queen, as temporal head of the Church of England, in a vulnerable position. By asking them to wait for a year it was possible the whole thing might solve itself.

After seeing the Queen Townsend decided to brave the Establishment in the person of Sir Alan 'Tommy' Lascelles, the Queen's private secretary. He regarded Lascelles as a friend and after telling him that he and Princess Margaret were in love and that, if necessary, he was ready to face the immediate consequences and leave the Queen Mother's household, he was deeply upset by the reaction. Remaining seated while Townsend stood nervously before him, Lascelles barked, 'You must be either mad or bad.' It was not

112

quite the response Townsend had expected. Though he knew he would not get sympathy, he had hoped for advice. But this was only the beginning. Opposition to him was building up among the Establishment diehards who treated him as though he had committed a crime.

Constitutionally the position was that under the Royal Marriages Act of 1772 Princess Margaret could not marry before her twenty-fifth birthday without the Queen's consent. The Act had been brought into being by George III, who had several dissolute sons likely to marry totally unsuitable women and he was only trying to preserve the Crown. However, as the Act had been passed it meant that even a twentieth-century princess had to submit to it. After the age of twenty-five she could marry without the Queen's consent but she would still need the consent of Parliament.

As the day of the Queen's coronation drew nearer every possible effort was made to keep the whole affair strictly within the family. No one, especially the two people most concerned, wanted to do anything that would distract attention from the historic climax of Elizabeth's life.

Though rumours had been circulating in the foreign press there had been no word in Britain of the potentially explosive love affair. On 2 June 1953, the day of the Coronation, American reporters, who had been told to keep their eyes open, saw Princess Margaret as Townsend described her, 'Superb, spark-ling, ravishing ... ', walk up to him, look deep into his eyes and brush a speck of fluff off his uniformed shoulder. Next day that feminine gesture, with its tender implications, made headlines in the New York press and in England *The People* followed up, breaking the silence and demanding to know what was happen-ing. Was Margaret going to be allowed to marry a divorced man? Did the British public know that scandalous rumours about the Princess were racing round the world?

From this moment on the private emotions of two people in love were considered unimportant set against the constitutional and religious aspects of the affair. Bellows of indignation were heard from all sides. Sir Winston Churchill pointed out that it would be disastrous for the Queen to even consider allowing her sister to marry a divorced man when she had only just been crowned. Parliament was against the match and it seemed unlikely that Princess Margaret would be given permission to marry by Westminster even after she was twenty-five. This she did not know. What she did know was that only by sacrificing everything could she become Peter Townsend's wife. That would mean renouncing her right of succession together with her income from the Civil List. She would then be simply Mrs Peter Townsend.

Both agreed that with the storm raging round them it would be better to separate for a short time. It came as a shock to Townsend when he discovered that plans had already been made to ensure they were kept apart. The Queen had been advised to send Townsend abroad immediately. Three posts were offered to him, one in Johannesburg, another in Singapore and a third in Brussels. As he had just been given custody of his two young sons, at boarding school in Kent, he chose Brussels and accepted the post of Air Attaché at the British Embassy. At least he would only be across the Channel. Townsend found the parting with his two young sons particularly harrowing. Hugo, then only eight, had seen newspaper headlines saying that his father was to be banished and thought he would never see him again.

Obviously sensing his unhappiness and remembering her father's affection for him, Queen Elizabeth would not allow him to be rushed out of the country. She had Townsend transferred to her own staff as an equerry and asked him to accompany her to Northern Ireland before taking up his post in Brussels.

The reality of his position became clear, however, when, at midday on 29 June, he went to Clarence House to take leave of the Queen Mother and Princess Margaret before they set off for a long-planned tour of Southern Rhodesia. Originally Townsend was to have accompanied them but his place had been taken by Lord Plunket. They said their farewells calmly because they fully expected to have a few days together when Margaret returned from Africa and before Townsend took up his appointment in Brussels. Things did not turn out that way.

Establishment powers behind the scenes were anxious to get rid of Peter Townsend as quickly as possible. Though he had been promised that he would not have to depart from England until after Princess Margaret's return, new orders were now given. He was hustled off to Brussels two days before the Rhodesia visit ended. 'Instead of our expected farewell, we were torn apart,' said Townsend. When the news was conveyed to Princess Margaret at the Leopard Rock Hotel in Umtali she succumbed to an attack of 'Bulawayo 'flu'. She was undoubtedly angry at the callous change in plans, obviously meant to separate her from Townsend as soon as possible, and her bitterness against the people she felt responsible lasted for a long time.

Both of them clung to the hope that they might be able to marry in two years time when Margaret would be twenty-five, and the Queen's consent no longer necessary. Once he had settled in at the British Embassy in Brussels, Townsend quickly took to the Belgians whom he found warm-hearted and generous. His diplomatic colleagues showed much kindness and he made friends quickly. But he still felt 'the loneliest man in Brussels'. He and Princess Margaret wrote to each other almost every day.

At home in England the official policy was to keep Princess Margaret busy, to keep her from brooding about that wretched fellow Townsend. She was allowed to distract herself with an amateur theatrical production of Edgar Wallace's *The Frog* at the Scala Theatre which starred a host of her friends and played to packed houses. Noel Coward was very rude about it, but it lifted the Princess out of her blue mood, and made £10,000 for the Invalid Childrens Aid Association. The following month she went to Germany, the first member of the royal family to pay an official visit for more than forty years. Finally she was given her first full-scale official overseas tour. The Queen had come up with an imaginative suggestion, a tour of the Caribbean – Trinidad, Jamaica, Barbados, Tobago, Antigua and Grenada. It would have been wonderful, Margaret told Peter, if only he had been coming with her. But in spite of her sad heart she was thrilled with the colour and gaiety of the calypso islands and returned with a deep sun-tan and a promise that she would visit them again one day. Eventually she was to build her own island home on Mustique, near St Vincent.

With the approach of Princess Margaret's twenty-fifth birthday on 21 August 1955 the media were galvanized into action and descended on Scotland in force. The royal family were at Balmoral as usual at this time of year, and there was a general feeling that something might be announced. Nothing happened, however. The Princess went to church at Crathie and Peter Townsend went to morning worship at the English church in Londonstraat in Ostende and said a prayer for them both.

That October, however, things began to move to a climax. Princess Margaret returned from Balmoral to London on

12 October and was seen to be in high spirits. The reason soon became clear. Peter Townsend had also arrived in London that day to spend a month's holiday in England. He was staying at the Marquess of Abergavenny's flat in Lowndes Square, Knightsbridge.

At 6.20 the following evening Townsend, at the wheel of his green Renault, drove to Clarence House for his first 'official' meeting with Princess Margaret for two years. He was almost blinded by flashbulbs as he drove through the gate where hundreds of pressmen and photographers were waiting. The Queen Mother left them alone. 'As we rediscovered one another, we realized that nothing had changed,' wrote Townsend. But he left again after one hour and forty minutes.

That weekend they were invited to stay with the Hon. Jean Wills, the Queen Mother's niece, and her husband Major Wills at their Georgian house, Allanby Park, in Berkshire. There was a little desultory socializing, a morning gallop, guests for tea. But most of the time was spent talking, trying to assess whether they had any reason to be at all hopeful. The next four days were spent in the company of good friends but sometimes they slipped away so that they could be alone together in Margaret's sitting-room at Clarence House.

The pressure was building up. While ninety per cent of ordinary British people and some of the tabloid papers were all for the marriage and said so, the various authorities were preparing for the final show-down. After a Cabinet meeting Sir Anthony Eden, the Prime Minister, saw the Queen and told her that Members of Parliament were hostile to any suggestion that Princess Margaret should retain her title on marriage. Not only would she lose her rank and her allowance but she would probably have to live abroad for some time. Various churchmen up and down the land said their piece and *The Times* weighed in with an appeal to Princess Margaret's conscience, arguing that a marriage with the divorced Townsend could not be regarded as a marriage at all by vast numbers of the Queen's people.

As the furore continued day after day the two people at the centre of it all began to lose heart. There was no doubt they were in love. But the onslaught was proving too much for them. Princessn Margaret had stood up well to the ordeal, quietly getting on with her job, remaining calm, but Townsend was beginning to show the strain. Eventually, as Christopher Warwick explains in his biography of Princess Margaret in which he drew on numerous conversations with her, 'Both Townsend and she felt thoroughly drained, thoroughly demoralized. They had reached a stage, in fact, where they could look at what lay before them dispassionately. This was the moment for Townsend to bow out of the Princess' life.'

When they met at Clarence House on the evening of 22 October both were mentally and physically exhausted. The arguments raging around them had become so fierce that they felt as though they were at the centre of a maelstrom. Princess Margaret spent the following weekend with the Queen and the Duke of Edinburgh at Windsor Castle. She made a telephone call to Townsend. 'She did not say what had passed between herself and her sister and brother-in-law,' he wrote, 'but doubtless the stern truth was dawning upon her.'

There is no doubt that both of them realized it was all over when they met once again at Clarence House on Monday, 24 October. Townsend knew in his heart that the sacrifices demanded of the Princess if she were to become his wife were too great; Margaret could not imagine life other than royal and was not prepared to take the way out chosen by her Uncle David, now exiled as the Duke of Windsor. They decided that if they could not marry openly, with full honours, they could not marry at all. Together they began to draft a statement that would tell the world of their decision. When it was finished they sat for a few moments looking at each other. 'There was a wonderful tenderness in her eyes,' Townsend wrote, 'which reflected, I suppose, the look in mine. We had reached the end of the road.'

Next morning Princess Margaret went to Lambeth Palace to see Dr Fisher, Archbishop of Canterbury. Thinking that she had come to see him about her marriage the Archbishop had spread around him books on historical precedent and canonical law. 'You can put your books away, Archbishop,' said the Princess. 'I have made up my mind already. I am not going to marry Peter Townsend.' She wanted him to be the first to know, the Church having been so implacably against the whole affair. Margaret then drove to Buckingham Palace where she told the Queen. She said she would be issuing a public statement which would make it clear that she still loved him.

Six days later, on Monday, 31 October 1955, as Princess

Margaret was photographed leaving Buckingham Palace, her face set, her eyes swollen with crying, this statement was issued:

> I would like it to be known that I have decided not to marry Group Captain Townsend. I have been aware that, subject to my renouncing my rights of succession, it might have been possible for me to contract a civil marriage. But mindful of the Church's teachings that Christian marriage is indissoluble, and conscious of my duty to the Commonwealth, I have resolved to put these considerations before others. I have reached this decision entirely alone and in doing so I have been strengthened by the unfailing support and devotion of Group Captain Townsend. I am deeply grateful for the concern of all those who have constantly prayed for my happiness.

Before they finally parted they spent a weekend together at Uckfield House in Sussex, home of Lord Rupert Nevill and his wife Anne, where they were seen walking hand-in-hand through the grounds of the estate. And on the day before he left for Brussels they had tea together at Clarence House, formally, and having said all there was to be said. While protesting to friends that it was a relief to have come to a decision, neither Margaret nor Townsend could conceal their unhappiness. They had been part of each other's life for nearly twelve years; it was unlikely that their paths would ever cross again.

Peter Townsend went back to Brussels but could not settle to his job as Air Attaché. He wanted to break away completely for a time and, to do so, took himself off on a journey round the world. He was to find future happiness in Belgium when he married Marie-Luce Jamagne, the daughter of friends he had known since he first went to Brussels. Princess Margaret too found happiness for a time when she married Anthony Armstrong-Jones, the brilliant photographer later to become Lord Snowdon. They met about two years after her dramatic decision and quickly became good friends. He introduced her to a world of clever, fascinating, artistic people; showed her life as she had hardly glimpsed it before. He took her secretly to his riverside retreat overlooking the Thames at Rotherhithe and arranged romantic candlelit dinners for the two of them at his basement studio flat in Pimlico. Their love affair did not become public property until the official announcement of their engagement, when Tony gave her a ring specially made to his own design – a ruby like a rosebud set in a marguerite of diamonds. Margaret had suffered so much from media coverage during the Townsend drama that it was decided not to reveal her new love too soon.

Their wedding at Westminster Abbey was celebrated with great national rejoicing and in the years that followed the births of their two children, Viscount Linley and Lady Sarah Armstrong-Jones, seemed to set the seal on a marriage that had caught the public's imagination. But Princess Margaret's happiness was not to last. By a cruel irony, twenty-three years after she had made her brave declaration in 1955, her marriage ended and she became the innocent party in a sad divorce.

# Crown Prince of Sikkim
## —AND—
# Hope Cooke

The story of Hope Cooke and the King of Sikkim has all the ingredients of a poignant modern fairy tale. It is about a young American girl, a New York student, who in 1963 married the heir-apparent of a tiny Himalayan kingdom thinking she had found a paradise on earth only, alas, to discover that fairy tales cannot always have happy endings in the ruthless political world of today.

Sikkim is now reduced to being the twenty-second state of India but when Hope Cooke first went there it seemed to her like the legendary Shangri La. Perched on 'the roof of the world' with the mighty, snow-clad peaks of Everest and Kanchenjunga soaring above its monasteries and temples, its foothills a profusion of rhododendrons and wild orchids, prayer flags fluttering against an azure sky, the ancient kingdom had a beauty that took her breath away.

She fell in love with Sikkim the moment she saw it, just as she had fallen in love with the tall, handsome man who was then Sikkim's Crown Prince and who would one day make her his queen. She was bowled over by the natural beauty of the country and its people. It did not seem like a strange land to her. In fact, she felt that she had been wandering for a long, long time and had at last come home.

If the residents of Sikkim, who regarded strangers with polite suspicion, were somewhat startled to learn that their Prince Palden Thondup Namgyal intended to take an American bride, her friends and relatives were not entirely surprised that something like this should happen to Hope. She was *different*, slightly mystical and poetic, always leaning towards the exotic. Ever since

121

she was a child her mind had been on faraway places.

She never knew her parents. They were divorced and her mother died when she was only two years old. She and her sister, Harriet, were brought up in New York by her grandparents who were wealthy and kind but who had no wish to allow little girls to interfere with their comfortable routine. Their own apartment on 62nd Street, between Park and Madison Avenues, was large and luxurious but when another across the hall became vacant they took it so that Hope and her sister could be raised there unseen and unheard and with the minimum of fuss.

Hope loved her grandparents' apartment. It was full of Far Eastern furniture and paintings. The dining-room had hand-painted Japanese wallpaper and there were ivory carvings and crystal balls from China. The living-room had a vast blue Chinese carpet. To her, it was like the sea, and she imagined herself bobbing off on its tiny blue waves to faraway lands in the big, model Chinese junk that stood on the bookcase.

When her grandparents died Hope was sent as a boarder to one of the classy, upper-crust girls' schools in New York and her Uncle Seldon and Aunt Mary were made her official guardians. Hope was quite excited about being put in their care. Seldon Chapin was a diplomat of the first order, who had been thrown out of Hungary for giving sanctuary to Cardinal Mindszenty. He was always, Hope thought, going or coming back from somewhere exotic.

The trouble was that Seldon Chapin had now been sent to Iran as U.S. Ambassador and no precise arrangements had been made for her in the holidays. Every free weekend and casual break became a time of apprehension and shame for the fifteen-year-old as she tried to scrounge invitations to fill in her time. Everybody, including the Chapins, she felt, must have forgotten about her. But in the summer of 1956, just when her teenage despair was at its lowest ebb, her guardians sent for her to spend the holidays with them in Teheran. It was to be her first experience of the East, her first step towards Asia. Her plane landed at Teheran in the pre-dawn out of a luminous dark-blue sky, the colour of stained glass. From the first moment the sights and sounds of Iran held her in thrall – the rose gardens and minarets, arab music coming from dark, cool interiors, the smell of spices and ripe apricots, the constant splash of fountains.

Life was a whirl of parties, barbecues and picnics, though most of them were with the same diplomatic set and the Iranian élite. Sometimes she would slip away and go for long walks around the suburbs of Teheran, yearning to know what was going on inside the maze of walled dwellings but still getting no nearer to the Iran she wanted to discover for herself.

The second year she returned to spend the summer in Iran she felt she had 'come home'. She dreaded returning to her boarding-school at the end of the holidays with its 'bleak dormitories of stupid girls' and weekends with nothing to do. The idea horrified her. 'Please let me stay,' she begged the Chapins, and they agreed. She was sent to a co-ed school where Americans, Iranians, Italians, Iraqis and Armenians all studied together. Bouffant skirted, her rich brown hair cut fashionably short around her face, she felt she had really grown up. Life was full to the brim. But while she listened as avidly as the other students to records of Elvis Presley, America seemed a world away. It was the realization that she was starting to fulfil her destiny that excited her when she woke each morning.

Hope had been on conventional trips to Persepolis, Shiraz and Isfahan but John Bowling, a friend in the American foreign service who tended to despise the usual run of poolside parties and had climbed in the Hindu Kush, offered to take her into the heart of Iran. Mounted on mules trammelled in brass bells and blue beads to ward off the evil eye, they crossed the interior, camping at night under the stars, each step an adventure. In her autobiography, *Time Change*, Hope Cooke describes reaching their destination, a White Russian pension in Babol Sar, a decaying town on the Caspian Sea, and says: 'I know this is close, very close, if not the exact route I want to be taking. I'm stormed by happiness, happiness for what I have and for the adventure I can't articulate which I know lies just beyond.'

The following spring Aunt Mary took Hope on a diplomatic jaunt to India and in Delhi she nearly exploded with excitement at the colour and beauty around her. From that moment on she sought out everything and everyone vaguely connected with India and to the amusement of her friend, John Bowling, dived with seventeen-year-old ardour into the study of Indian religions. She felt she had to stay close to India some way or other.

News that her Uncle Seldon was leaving Teheran to take up

another post in the West appalled her. She could not go back. But plans had already been made for her to finish her education at the prestigious Sarah Lawrence College in Bronxville, New York, and though her heart felt as though it was breaking there was no alternative. Shortly after her eighteenth birthday all her friends accompanied her to the airport. They embraced her, pressed small gifts into her hands and begged her not to forget, not ever to forget. She could hardly breathe for sadness.

As a Sarah Lawrence student she applied to take a course in Asian history but there was not one available to a fresher. She took European history instead and read books on Hinduism and Buddhism every spare minute. She became somewhat eccentric though extremely pretty. Her brown hair, now grown to her waist, was usually twisted into a huge bun on top of her head. She outlined her eyes in black like a Persian houri but otherwise disdained make up. Totally disinterested in clothes, she tended to live in three outfits, her favourite items of clothing being a sari for summer, Iranian sheepskin leggings for winter and a voluminous Afghan tent-dress for special occasions. She skipped meals, living mostly on ice cream. Once, invited to a party, she wore her grandmother's priceless sables – and went home without them.

During the summer of 1959 plans were made for a group of Sarah Lawrence history students to visit Russia. Hope Cooke decided the experience would round out and help her studies and put her name down for the trip. But she had no intention of returning home once the Russian tour was over. She had had a wonderful idea. From there she could fly on to India and spend the rest of the summer in Asia. Her Aunt Mary would think she was still with a group and wouldn't object, though she would no doubt have vetoed any idea of Hope going to India alone.

She knew several families in Delhi and felt sure she could stay with one of them. Arriving in India, however, she found most of them about to leave for their holidays in Europe and America, and her heart sank at the thought of what her guardians would say if they found out. Where to go next? She remembered leafing through a travel agent's brochure and finding that the most sedate and Englishy hotel in the whole of India seemed to be the Windemere in Darjeeling. Purchasing a first-class rail ticket, she set off for the hill station in North Bengal, sitting next to an old Bengali lady who fussed over her like a mother hen.

Darjeeling in some ways was still a ghostly relic of earlier times when English tea-planters and their ladies waltzed at the club balls and the memsahibs and their offspring fled there to escape the heat of the plains. But what fascinated Hope Cooke was the fact that it was also the point at which Nepalese, Sikkimese and Tibetans converged, being the highest administrative frontier town to those remote Himalayan countries.

She watched the comings and goings from the safe, chintzy comfort of the Windemere but sometimes felt awkward being there alone. The couple who owned the hotel took her under their wing and sometimes their son, Kesang, offered to take her into the town to see some of the monasteries or else to escort her on weekend taxi-drives into the hills.

All sorts of visitors came and went through the main lounge of the hotel and she was fascinated by many of them. One afternoon, having arranged to go out, she was waiting there for a car. She had been invited to have tea with an expatriate Australian who was running a dairy farm that supplied cheese and hams throughout India. As she was about to depart Kesang called out to her, 'Please come, there is someone I want you to meet.'

She found herself looking up into the face of a tall, handsome man with smooth bronze skin, high cheekbones and dark, penetrating eyes. His mouth, she noticed, was beautifully shaped and sensual. For a few seconds she was lost for words, then realized that Kesang was introducing her to the Maharaj Kumar or Crown Prince of Sikkim.

Prince Palden Thondup Namgyal was a widower. His wife, a Tibetan princess, had died in childbirth and he had sent his two young sons to boarding-school in Darjeeling. It took him four hours to drive his blue Mercedes along the breathtakingly narrow road that led in repeated hairpin bends from his country's capital, Gangkok, to the outside world. In the few minutes they had to talk before Hope's car arrived she learned that the Prince was staying overnight at the hotel and they would meet again later in the day.

That night at dinner and afterwards he talked of the terrible things that had been happening in Tibet, now overrun by Communist China. Sikkim itself, he told her, was in a dangerous and vulnerable position, lying as it did on the frontier between

China and India. His father, the King, was an old and frail man and he felt responsible for his country. Hope listened with rapt attention, her eyes fixed on his face. The scene comes vividly to life in her autobiography. Leaning forward into the lamplight he went on, 'Back in the early Fifties when I tried to help Tibet, the only time they could be helped, the American government let me down.' He sighed. 'All we needed was a few planes. A few planes. Now they're helping this Johnny-come-lately crowd of Tibetan politicians – and what happens? The weapons all fall into Chinese hands and the Tibetans are killed.' She was struck by the sense of pain and loss which seemed to run through him; by his sensitive face which altered from sadness when he talked about Tibet to a puckish good humour when the subject was changed.

By next morning he had taken the road back to Gangkok. 'All that chap does is sit up in Sikkim,' Kesang said to her. 'Stays up there for months at a time without ever coming out. He's got too much sense of duty. They don't deserve him. A bloody monk's life he leads.' When he had gone back to his mountain kingdom she found she could not get him out of her mind. The remaining weeks of the summer passed quietly but she often looked to-wards the Himalayas and thought of him – his rueful, droll manner, his obvious integrity and his extraordinary, handsome looks. But they were not to meet again for two years.

Hope went back to Sarah Lawrence and immersed herself in studies and friendships. She acquired her first real boyfriend, Emile, an Illinois college drop-out who spent his whole life reading books on history and poetry. 'Walking the streets past the deserted stock exchange, warehouses, rotting piers and fish markets lit by oil-drum fires, we would spend the cold spring nights talking about poetry and Asia,' she wrote. Mostly, however, they would just lie on the llama-skin rug in her room, laughing, smoking and eating greasy take-away suppers.

She was due to 'come of age' in the summer of 1961 and, with Emile, planned a trip to Asia. She thought she would stop over in London to visit the School of Oriental and African studies, then pay a short visit to Darjeeling before meeting Emile in Iran. But she knew in her heart of hearts that the only part of the trip that mattered to her was Darjeeling and she would probably never go on to Iran. She had not heard from the Prince nor had she made any attempt to contact him. She was sensitive to the fact that this might be considered improper. Nevertheless, she confessed in a letter to a friend that she had experienced an attraction to this man for the past two years.

With mounting excitement she bought all the necessary tickets and wrote to the Windemere Hotel to tell them she was coming. After a journey that seemed to last for ever she was at last standing once more in its familiar, cosy foyer being greeted with joy by her friend Kesang. Not long afterwards she heard him on the telephone saying, 'She's here. She's come back,' and knew he was talking to the Maharaj Kumar.

One morning he walked into the hotel and asked for her – just materialized as though there had been no time in between. That night he took her to a military ball at the Gymkhana Club and people began to ask who was the lovely, slender American girl with coppery brown hair and a soft voice almost like a whisper.

Soon he arranged for a group of his Darjeeling friends to drive her out to see him in Gangkok. Hope's first sight of Sikkim filled her with emotion. For some reason she felt this was where she truly belonged. Flowers of every description grew in profusion beneath a sapphire-blue sky, cherry blossom and poinsettias flourishing side by side, orchids growing wild in the fields and dark-leaved trees bearing the sweetest oranges climbing the terraced hillsides. Even the dusty, ramshackle streets of old Gangkok were made vivid by the saffron robes of Buddhist monks. Above everything towered the great Himalayan peaks.

The Maharaj Kumar, she discovered, was far from being a simple man in spite of the remoteness of his country. He spoke flawless English as well as four other languages and his interests ranged from poetry to international politics. She was beginning to feel a stronger and stronger attraction to him. What also fascinated her was the fact that he had such a practical side to his nature and had literally helped to engineer a great deal of the development in Sikkim, from the modern orange-juice factory to the highly efficient Sikkim national transport system.

During this first visit the Prince introduced her to his three children and to his father, Sir Tashi Namgyal, King of Sikkim, who for twenty years had been a semi-invalid and recluse spending most of his time painting and meditating, leaving the running of the country to his son. She stayed in the royal guest house in the palace compound for six days.

127

During that summer they met as often as they could. Hope had never been happier in her life and, trusting her feelings, just allowed one week to flow into another without making any plans to return to America. He would drive down the mountain road in his Mercedes like someone coming from another world, sometimes taking her back with him to Gangkok. They felt, increasingly, they had to be together. 'We have a connection so close it is almost like a membrane joining us,' she wrote in her diary. 'Sometimes it seems that in an almost Buddhist way I've lost my ego and am becoming part of him.'

Watching the Prince with his children filled her with tenderness. 'The last time I was in Gangkok,' she wrote, 'he and his little girl, Yangchen Dolma, were doing prostrations in the chapel. I watched as, continuing his own prayers, he gently showed her how to fold her hands. I was so overcome with happiness and longing that I just stayed kneeling and couldn't get up on my feet.'

Hope's tendency to regard him as something of a saint – he had been trained as a Buddhist monk – both irked and amused the Crown Prince. He was determined to change her 'pure' image of him, to make her see him as a real man, one who had in the past been involved with many other women. But he also made it clear to her that she was becoming very special to him. As though to emphasize this he asked her to act as guardian to five-year-old Yangchen when she started boarding-school in Darjeeling.

She did not go too often to Gangkok. It would, she was warned by her close friends in Darjeeling, look too 'pushy'. She had to be very careful. American girls were regarded as very easy and promiscuous by some of the locals, who got most of their ideas from the rather steamy films on show at the local cinema. So she waited patiently for him to visit her in the sedate and proper atmosphere of the Windemere. 'When he comes down here, life is wonderful but otherwise it's pretty dreary,' she noted in her diary. When he took her back with him to Sikkim for a weekend they would spend the evenings dancing close together on the rose-coloured carpet in his drawing-room and playing records from his huge collection of European classics.

The night he asked her to marry him he came down to Darjeeling with a band of Indian army officers and announced they were all going to the ball at the Gymkhana Club. 'He was prancing about like Peter Pan with the lost boys. I felt like Wendy.' As they were dancing he whispered in her ear and Hope answered fervently, 'Yes, yes, yes.'

They were engaged in November 1961 at a simple ceremony in the palace with the King, the Prime Minister and a few other dignitaries present. She was touched by the kindness and open mindedness of the old King who had replied, when his son had asked if he minded him marrying an American girl, 'Do whatever makes you happy.' They exchanged long white scarves, symbols of peace and friendship, and the Prince slipped a diamond ring on to her finger, giving her a teasing glance from his long, dark eyes as he said most girls in the West expected one.

She would always remember a tender moment between them before the ceremony began. The Prince walked down to the guest house to fetch her. The sun was pouring into the room and she could hear the river rippling below the window and the muffled sound of Tibetan horns from the monastery. She was ready, except for one thing. Her fingers had developed sores, which she had neglected, and she found it difficult to bandage them herself. He sat on the bed and gently bound them up for her, teasing her about whether there was space, or indeed a finger, left for the engagement ring. 'It was a tender time and very like him, concerned with such small, practical things as bandages.' He told her he did not really like manicured people, and smart American women with big hands and varnished nails appalled him.

On the advice of the astrologers the Prince's sister was being married on the day of their engagement, the auspices, apparently, being particularly good. So once the ring was on Hope's finger they had to hurry off to her reception. Afterwards everyone let their hair down Sikkimese style and played hide-and-seek round the palace, followed by the kite-tail game in which everyone hung on to someone else, the leader trying by curving and whipping back and forth to throw off whoever was clinging on at the end. Hope joined in with glee, her happiness so complete she said a prayer: 'Please God, don't give me anything else – but don't take anything away.'

Once the announcement of her engagement had appeared in the *New York Times* life became very different for Hope. She found herself the object of immense curiosity and began to 'feel like public property'. She discovered that a Bengali tycoon and his wife had booked into the Windemere Hotel just so that they could have a close look at her. 'They examined me so closely I thought they were going to make an inventory.' Some local Tibetans were spreading rumours that she was a whore and she even heard suggestions that she was working for the C.I.A. and the marriage was a political put-up job.

Royal astrologers in Sikkim proclaimed that 1962 was an inauspicious year for marriage, so it was decided that Hope should go back to America, finish her studies and settle her affairs. At Sarah Lawrence she found it difficult to jerk her mind back to the world of girlish confessions in the dorm, junk food and heavy dates. Missing the man she loved, not too certain of his idea of fidelity and longing for the mountains, she neglected herself during the final term of studies and fell a victim to hepatitis. The Prince flew to New York immediately news reached him that she was ill. Sweeping aside hints that had reached her in letters from her friend Kesang that he had been seeing an American called Grace Baines who had turned up in Darjeeling as 'something of a mountain climber and painter', he assured her, 'I love you. Don't forget you're my woman and soon will be my wife.' All the same, the Baines woman rankled.

The wedding was fixed for 20 March 1963. Hope made arrangements for her own precious bits of furniture and personal belongings to be shipped to India where they would be taken overland to Sikkim. She bought presents in New York for her new family, suitcases of toys for little Yangchen and the Prince's two sons, Wongchuk and Tenzing. For the first time in her life she went to the hairdresser to have her long brown hair coiffured and sprayed with lacquer before facing the barrage of press cameras at the airport. At the stopover in Karachi she slipped out of her smart, tailored shirtwaister and into a long silken Sikkimese robe.

The wedding was a brilliant, exotic, chaotic affair at which Western guests and photographers could hardly take in the vivid colour and dramatic imagery at every corner they turned. Buddhist priests in their russet and saffron robes with horns, cymbals and drums mingled with people from every Himalayan tribe, each in their own costume, and soldiers in full-dress scarlet coats seemed to be everywhere. Hope struggled into a traditional

Sikkimese brocade wedding dress wrapped tightly around her slender figure and secured with a silver belt. A Polish hairdresser had been brought all the way from Calcutta to pile her hair on top of her head and fix it with lacquer. She set off for the ceremony fortified by half a Valium tablet pressed upon her by a nervous American guest.

As she walked through the doorway of the royal chapel, peering into the dark interior she became fully aware for the first time that she was marrying a senior reincarnation, a man who was Buddhist by birth and training and whose family had ruled in this place for 325 years. Gliding along the polished floor, aware of the tightness of her dress, she paused to light butter lamps in front of the images of Buddha and the guru who had brought Buddhism to Tibet and Sikkim in the eighth century. As each wick flickered into life she made a silent vow to herself to make this marriage happy.

Before going to sit on the gilded, carved throne next to the Crown Prince, she reached up to the high throne where her father-in-law, the old King, sat looking frail and isolated and, with a shy smile, handed him the traditional white silk scarf. The King smiled down at her fondly. Having lit the lamps and offered the scarf, her part in the ceremony was virtually over. All she had to do was sit quietly at her husband's side with the heavy gold and purple ceremonial cape embroidered with dragons over her shoulders. Half way through, as she listened to the court music-ians singing in high, reedy voices 'a flower of the West blossoms among us', she caught her husband's eye. Smiling mischievously, he tossed her a plain gold wedding ring. It was not something that usually happened at Sikkimese weddings, but the intimacy of the gesture obviously pleased them both.

Celebrations went on for a week, not a long time for a party in the Himalayas, but Hope wished everyone would go away so that she could begin her married life. The palace which was now to be her home was not splendid by royal standards. Built in 1910, it was a rambling, two-storey building with white stucco walls, a red corrugated iron roof, five bedrooms, verandahs and spacious gardens. Apart from the Prince's living-room with its glowing rose carpet, books and magnificent views, the rest of the place had been neglected for years. Even the bedrooms were dark and gloomy, one of them reputed to be haunted, and some parts of the house, little used, had languished under a film of cobwebs and dust. Hope settled down to redecorating with the zeal of an all-American housewife.

During the day she tended to wear sweaters and long corduroy skirts but when guests arrived or when she appeared in public she put on a Sikkimese *kho*, the traditional dress which was like a long silky jumper wrapped around the body and tied over a contrasting blouse, both in vivid, jewel colours. Her obvious love and enthusiasm for her adopted country quickly endeared her to many people. Her most difficult task was being accepted by the Prince's sister, Cocoola, who 'full of anger and hard as a diamond' had lost her home in Tibet and with it her status as a princess. She had been running the household for him and had to be handled with extreme delicacy.

There was no such difficulty about the royal children. From the very beginning they had loved her and she adored them, especially little Yangchen, who had written to her in America: 'Please come home to us.' She felt a great sadness when her husband decided to send his sons, Wongchuk and Tenzing, to be educated in England. She missed them terribly and the rambling old house seemed empty without them.

Only a year after their marriage the old King died and Prince Palden Thondup Namgyal succeeded to the throne of Sikkim. He was addressed as 'Chogyal', the ancient Tibetan title for a ruler, and Hope became the 'Gyalmo', though she was, more often than not, addressed as Queen Hopla.

The coronation filled her with awe. She was elaborately dressed in red and gold Chinese brocade but the splendour surrounding her husband seemed to set him apart and gave him an aura of mystery that almost made him a stranger. Spectacular in gold dragon robes, his face a bronze, impassive mask, he crowned himself with the ancient fur crown of his ancestors. He spoke passionately from the throne promising to make Sikkim a paradise and swearing he would not rest until every last bit of want and ignorance was swept from the land.

Hope's life changed overnight. Her official duties doubled. She was expected to organize the servants at the palace and supervize their work. She had to plan menus for state dinners, look after the well-being of a continual flow of diplomatic guests and keep the palace larder suitably stocked, not an easy job as most supplies had to be ordered from outside the country.

During his years as Crown Prince, the King had already done a great deal to try to bring Sikkim into the twentieth century and the standard of living was higher than in any other Himalayan kingdom, with good roads, free medicine, a reliable bus service and modern schools. But many of his subjects lived in scattered, isolated villages difficult to get to with any transport, and he spent part of each year visiting them on foot. Now he wanted Hope to go with him.

Sikkim was often devastated by monsoon rains which caused landslides and flood damage and the appearance of the two of them after this kind of disaster was very important. They would stay in tents and local bungalows, listen to complaints and promise help. Hope, addressed as 'Queen of the happy valley' and 'Consort of deities', was regarded at first with narrow-eyed suspicion which soon turned to merry curiosity.

The King was often away from the palace on political and business trips and then she sometimes felt loneliness creeping up on her. To fill her time she made it her special concern to encourage the development of native arts and crafts; to revive the long-dormant cottage industry of Sikkim, persuading people to make things that were simple and beautiful according to centuries-old tradition rather than copying the cheap commercial Indian goods that flooded the tourist market.

Visiting journalists, friends and diplomats who sometimes drifted up from Darjeeling went away with the feeling that the marriage was working well. They noticed the delightful gestures of affection and intimacy, the private jokes and moments of loving concern. But as the years went by Hope found that one of the unavoidable penalties of being the wife of the King of Sikkim was the loss of intimacy and privacy. The evenings when they found themselves alone, without official duties, became rare.

The birth of their son, Palden, followed by that of their almond-eyed daughter, Hope Leezum, brought them great joy. The King was a loving and attentive father to all his children. On the occasions when they were all together as a family the palace came alive and it did not seem possible that anything could spoil what they had. There was such merriment and laughter, such love and affection.

Periodically the royal family made trips to New Delhi and for two months of the year travelled abroad. But all such journeys had to start from Calcutta, at least a day away from Gangkok by car and plane, and had to be planned well in advance. Their appearance in the Western world was usually accompanied by crowds of reporters and flash bulbs as Queen Hope from Seal Island, Maine, was still regarded as a good story.

Rumblings of trouble to come in their Himalayan paradise were heard soon after the coronation. The Chinese were threatening to take over the border they shared with Sikkim at the Nathu Pass on the edge of what was once Tibet. It was only twenty miles from Gangkok. As Sikkim had been an Indian protectorate since 1950, Indian troops were rushed to the Pass and danger was averted. But the King was not happy to see so many Indian soldiers in his country. It reminded him of how hard he would have to struggle to remain independent politically because of Sikkim's vulnerable position as a buffer state between India and China.

Hope prayed that their friendship with the Indian premier, Mrs Gandhi, would keep them safe. She had, after all, been to their wedding and had furnished her house with craft work from Sikkim. The King went to see Mrs Gandhi but was not sure he had 'got through'.

Year by year there seemed to be more evidence of unrest around Gangkok. Agitators were urging the people to press for electoral reform. By 1972 it was evident that trouble was in the air. Hope begged the King to tell her what was going wrong; he said intelligence reports had been citing evidence of a plot to cause widespread disturbance in Sikkim and that stocks of ammunition had already been smuggled into the country by trouble makers.

There were hints of trouble of a far more personal kind, too. Though she was sure the King loved her, Hope knew that his attention often strayed. She suffered agonies of jealousy over Grace Baines and knew that she had been writing to him for years. Sometimes she could feel the crisp, rustling paper she used tucked into his sash when she went to hug him. 'It is nothing', he would say dismissively. Her own emotions were put to the test when an old friend from her schooldays in America, a writer, turned up in the Himalayas on a travel assignment. She seemed to be able to communicate with him in a direct way she had forgotten. She saw him again when she visited New York, and for the first time ever when she returned to Sikkim she felt strained, on edge.

All this was pushed into the background when on 20 March 1973, the tenth anniversary of their wedding, the first demonstrations against the monarchy took place in Gangkok. Hope was appalled to see photographs of herself and the King burned in the streets. The violence escalated. News came through that police stations in south, east and west Sikkim had been overrun, looted and arms stolen. That night the King slept with a loaded gun next to his painting of the Buddha.

In the days that followed the sound of chanting mobs could be heard coming closer and closer to the palace and both Hope and the children were gripped by a wave of fear. 'Today in town the Indian army stood by while crowds looted the police station and our own police, whom they've demobilized, had to stand by and watch. The King is enraged by the Indians' breach of faith', wrote Hope in her diary.

The royal family was virtually imprisoned in the palace at Gangkok from the beginning of April until the third week in May while riots broke out spasmodically and demonstrators poured over the border from India. News reached them that about five or six thousand loyal Sikkimese from the north were on the march with long swords to defend their country against the rioters and save their King. The thought filled the King with dread, for the Indian army was coming in armed with grenades, guns and mortars.

Once the Indians had gained control the siege was lifted. The ancient monarchy of Sikkim had come to an end. To Hope's distress the press reports they saw concentrated on their downfall, describing the King as inept and nothing more than the descendant of a Tibetan bandit and herself as a domineering, ambitious woman who had gained a terrible hold on him. But in Europe and America informed opinion was saying that the government in New Delhi had simply wanted to tighten its grip on an area it considered crucial to its defence. Mr and Mrs Namgyal, as they now were, were just unfortunate victims.

Hope's feelings were numbed. Her husband was overcome with grief and pain at the takeover of his country and hardly seemed to know she existed. She felt she could not leave him yet, though there did not seem to be a future for them in Sikkim.

One day she received an anonymous letter signed 'Black April' threatening to tear her and her children to pieces if they set foot outside the palace. Smallpox had broken out in Gangkok, brought in probably by the thousands of demonstrators from over the border. Sikkim had been free of the disease for many years. Hope knew in her heart that the only way for herself and her children to survive was to return to America and find a temporary home and a school. It had been discovered that Yangchen had kidney trouble. It would be an opportunity for her to receive treatment. The King, however, was under house arrest and would have to stay.

Their farewell was full of anguish, for both knew that it was the beginning of the end of their marriage. It was something that had belonged to the old Sikkim, before the troubles, and now they were drifting apart.

Embracing her husband for the last time she whispered, 'I am coming back. I am coming back in a few weeks.' When she reached Bombay she rang the palace and spoke to him: 'I won't go, I'll come back.' Wearily he said that, as she had got so far, she had better go on with the children, then reconsider her plans.

For the whole of the first year in America she still believed she would return. She received long, heartbreaking letters from the palace in Gangkok but they were all about the loss of his country and the death of his dreams for Sikkim. To her horror one letter told of the death of twenty-six-year-old Tenzing. He had been driving the palace car on a road built for one-way traffic and was hit by a truck coming in the opposite direction.

Hope had settled with the children at Martha's Vineyard in Massachusetts, where she tried to build a new life for herself. Part of her still belonged to Sikkim and she welcomed every visitor who came bringing a breath of the Himalayas. One summer the Rinpoche, a senior priest of Sikkim who spent part of each year in America teaching Buddhism, stayed with her and, gathering his russet robes around him, swam in the sea for the first time in his life. She was determined that her children, Palden and Hope Leezum, should never lose their Sikkimese roots. She cooked dishes for them that she used to order for the King in happier days so that they could have a taste of 'home'. Wistfully she remembered how when her husband had wanted to relax or forget his political troubles he would merrily invade the palace kitchen, put on a huge apron and, with a skill that surprised her, prepare delicious rice and traditional Himalayan food. Hope would sit with her guests by candlelight until the early hours, talking about the country they had loved so much.

Hope and her husband met once again in New York. Having signed a paper recognizing the application of India's constitution to Sikkim, he had been given permission to travel abroad. She took the children to New York to see him and they arranged to make their separation final. Whatever happened in the future, their personal dream was over.

# Princess Margaretha
## —AND—
# Robin Douglas-Home

On certain nights of the week in the 1950s a fair-haired, good-looking young man in a white dinner-jacket could be found quietly playing romantic tunes at a white piano at either the Casanova Club or the Berkeley Hotel in London's West End.

There was something about him that made even the casual observer realize that he was not in the ordinary run of nightclub piano players. Perhaps it was the clear-cut, aristocratic profile, the quiet, cultured voice, or the fact that he was greeted familiarly by many of the rich young people who drifted in and out in search of an evening's entertainment.

One night in 1957 a party arrived at the Casanova Club just as he was starting to play his opening tune, 'I'm in the Mood for Love'. Among the bright young socialites ordering champagne he saw one girl whose sparkling eyes, sun-tanned skin and dazzling smile made her stand out from the rest.

The beautiful girl was Princess Margaretha of Sweden. Soon it became obvious that the interest was mutual. The pianist was invited to join the party and before long the two were deep in conversation. They found they had friends in common, among them Princess Alexandra of Kent. The pianist asked the Princess if she would care to join him for dinner one night. She answered yes, and that was the beginning of a bitter-sweet romance that haunted the gossip columns for two years – until it ended as intriguingly as it had begun.

The piano player was Robin Douglas-Home, twenty-five, old Etonian, nephew of the fourteenth Earl of Home – one day to be Britain's Prime Minister – and a member of the group which became known as 'the Princess Margaret Set'. He had all the right credentials except one. He was by no means rich and had to work to keep up the lifestyle which he felt was expected of him. During the day he was a copy-writer in a London advertising firm. In the evening he changed into his white dinner-jacket and used his undoubted talent as a pianist to play romantic tunes.

His image as a nightclub piano player was, therefore, rather deceptive. There was much more to Robin Douglas-Home than that. He was an aristocrat of impeccable background, educated at one of Britain's most exclusive preparatory schools, Ludgrove in Berkshire, before going to Eton. His father was Major Henry Douglas-Home, a distinguished ornithologist who had a fine Army career. Robin himself served as an intelligence officer in the Seaforth Highlanders after Eton. He was in the Army for five years but resigned his commission after a row at the War Office over what he regarded as indifference to the death of a member of his platoon in an ambush in South Arabia. Friends suggested that the row had really been engineered by Robin because he could not stand military life and wanted to get out.

He arrived in London's West End in the early Fifties and became part of the Princess Margaret crowd. He fitted in beautifully with his old-world courtesy and impeccable manners. He was a sensitive man, artistic, attentive, the type who took girls to tea at the Ritz. Within a short time he was a favourite with Princess Margaret. He was usually around when 'the Set' got together at places like the Stork Room, and Princess Margaret often asked for him to be invited to house parties. She would send her car to pick him up in London so that they could drive to the country. She loved to sing popular songs while he played the piano.

Robin became a copy-writer to supplement his income and first appeared as a pianist at Rico Dajou's Casanova Club in Grosvenor Street, where he played to debutantes and their titled boyfriends, most of whom he knew socially. They crowded in to hear him run through his repertoire of romantic songs. He really preferred jazz. His lack of wealth certainly made no difference to his attraction for the opposite sex and, anyway, he always believed that success was just around the corner.

After their first encounter Princess Margaretha started going to the club and to the Berkeley Hotel specially to meet him. It all remained a very discreet affair within the hot-house atmosphere in which they both moved. They made a handsome couple, twenty-three-year-old Margaretha vivacious and beautiful in the Scandinavian way; Robin, slim and blond, with his pale, romantic, Leslie Howard looks. One night, however, the fact that they were falling in love was revealed to the whole world. When Robin took Princess Margaretha in his arms to dance a photographer, who had been lying in wait, caught the look that passed between them. Next morning it was all over the national press. Robin was furious. He had already been invited to visit Sweden and felt that the publicity might upset the Swedish royal family.

There was no doubt that the news that Princess Margaretha was in love with a young aristocrat who played the piano in night-clubs caused a great deal of consternation in the palace in Stockholm. While most Swedes thought it was rather a good idea for their pretty, democratic Princess to marry an Englishman with good connections, her mother, Princess Sybilla, thought otherwise.

Ever since her husband Crown Prince Gustav Adolf had been killed in a plane crash in 1947, leaving her with four mettlesome daughters and a son to bring up, Princess Sybilla had not had an easy time. The death of Gustav had created a gap in the royal succession. Now she would never be queen. She was not related to the Swedish royal family either by blood or nationality. She was German, a Saxe-Coburg-Gotha, and without Gustav at her side she felt sometimes as though she had been left stranded. Her one ambition now was to see her daughters marry well. She was especially concerned about Margaretha, her eldest daughter, and hoped that one day she might marry King Baudouin of Belgium. Now there was this young English aristocrat with no money formally asking her to accept him as her daughter's suitor.

Considered by the standards of other royals in Europe, Princess Margaretha was not wealthy. She had been brought up in the democratic Scandinavian manner, had an ordinary school education and was left free, like all the children of the Swedish royal family, to follow her own particular interests. Swedes were used to seeing Margaretha shopping and having lunch in Stockholm without an escort. She took a domestic science course and showed a great fondness for children, which, together with her pleasant manner and lovely wide smile, endeared her to the Swedish people.

As she grew into young womanhood, however, she had a hankering to see something of the glamorous life in a wider world. The city of her dreams was not Paris or Rome but London where she knew Princess Margaret led an established circle of young royals who knew how to enjoy themselves. Margaretha knew Princess Alexandra and through her was able to slip into the mainstream of London society in the Fifties, so meeting Robin Douglas-Home.

All through that year they were frequently seen dining and dancing together in exclusive clubs and restaurants in the West End, and sometimes Robin held discreet little parties at his bachelor flat in Onslow Gardens, Kensington. There was no doubt that he was hoping desperately that he would be successful in his courtship and would ultimately win Margaretha's hand in marriage. When he went home for Christmas in 1957 he told his father that he loved Margaretha, that she loved him, and that he wished to marry her. Major Douglas-Home advised him to 'get something sorted out with the Swedish royal family as soon as possible'. The Princess herself had by now returned home.

At last, in February 1958, came the call from Stockholm that Robin had been waiting for. Princess Sybilla sent a formal invitation. The visit, to take place in March, was announced in a Swedish Court communiqué and brought predictions in London and Stockholm that their engagement would soon be announced. But the communiqué did not mention an engagement. It merely said that the nephew of the Earl of Home would be going to Sweden to tour the Esselte printing works and that he would meet Princess Margaretha.

Suddenly there was immense interest in the possibility of a marriage. Princess Alexandra, known to be a friend of both, would only say, 'I cannot make any statement until the Swedish Court has something to say,' but others were not so reticent. Robin's mother Lady Margaret, at her flat in Onslow Square, said happily that she hoped her son would marry Princess Margaretha 'this year'. Even in Stockholm Admiral Wetter, the royal Court Marshal, ventured to say: 'The King has decided that an announcement is to be made about Robin Douglas-Home's engagement to Princess Margaretha. I cannot tell you at this time what the decision is, but we in Sweden are happy about it.' One Swedish evening newspaper even went so far as to say that the King had given his grand-daughter permission to marry. Certainly it was known that Sweden's Prime Minister, Dr Tage Erlander, had discussed the romance with Queen Elizabeth when he had an audience with her on a visit to London. He dined with the Swedish Ambassador, Mr Gunnar Hagglof, in London one night before going on to a ball that was being given for debutantes Marina and Tessa Kennedy. The invitation to the Swedish Embassy was considered to have great significance at this stage of his romance with Princess Margaretha for it showed in diplomatic circles that he was considered *persona grata*. One gossip columnist who attended the ball reported overhearing a conversation between Robin and Princess Alexandra. She turned to him and said, 'Robin, I've heard and read a great deal about you in the last few days. Is it all true?' He replied with a whimsical smile, 'I've been asked this by many people. Shall we dance....'

Meanwhile his mother, Lady Margaret, was telling reporters, 'I hope that the end of this matter brings joy to them both because one day, if things were to be as people say, Princess Margaretha would be my daughter-in-law.' She admitted that Robin had never discussed the Princess with her – 'he has always been too shy' – nor had she met the lovely girl with whom her son was so much in love. That would perhaps come later. As for rumours that the Swedish royals did not approve of Robin's lifestyle, she said proudly, 'My son is worthy of any girl, princess or commoner.' Things seemed all set for a happy future. But, as it turned out, too many people were jumping the gun.

According to plan, in March Robin Douglas-Home set off for Sweden to try to win his princess. It was fully expected by many people that an engagement would be announced the following week. He flew into Stockholm under the name of Mr York, hoping to escape publicity, but he was given full V.I.P. treatment. The entire British Embassy staff turned out to meet him.

Stockholm was under deep snow and for six days on that winter visit Robin saw his princess every single day. It was obvious to everyone that they were in love, but by the time the visit was over Margaretha was in tears and it was a very subdued suitor who boarded the plane home.

King Gustav himself had liked the young man and told him that he would put no obstacle in the way of an engagement if they were absolutely certain of their feelings. He adored his grand-daughter and only wanted her happiness. But the atmosphere in the royal palace was tense. The main opposition, it is believed, came from Princess Sybilla, who did not take to the cool, fair-haired Englishman. It was made quite clear that his way of life was not considered to be particularly stable and he was not thought to be in a position to support the Princess in the manner to which she had been accustomed. None of the royal Swedish princesses had a fortune of her own but anyone wishing to marry them ought to be able to provide them with the basic luxuries. Perhaps, it was suggested, he should try to find a career that would present him in a more favourable light; then he could ask for her hand again.

Robin returned to England looking downcast, with no engagement announcement imminent. But he took to heart the advice about improving his image and joined the wealthy Jocelyn Stevens and Shaun, brother of Lord Plunket, Deputy Master of the Royal Household, in a publishing business specializing in industrial matters. It was not really to Robin's liking but he thought it ought to please Margaretha's relatives.

On leaving Stockholm he had told reporters, 'Whatever happens, I shall return.' His next visit was planned for May but he caught jaundice and had to postpone it. Princess Sybilla suggested he should join them at her summer palace, Solliden Castle on the island of Oleand, in July. The lovers continued to keep in touch by constant telephone calls but were undoubtedly miserable about the delicate delaying tactics that were going on around them. He kept a low profile through this period as he felt that any fresh outburst of publicity would bring another round of obstacles into the path of their engagement and marriage. The gossip columns were full of speculation, Robin complained that his romance was being turned into a circus by the newspapers and he knew the effect some of the stories would have on the Swedish royal family.

Princess Margaretha in Sweden was deeply upset by rumours that she had quarrelled with Robin. The delay in arranging his next visit, explained Count Goesta Lewenhaupt, the Court Chamberlain, was simply because the Princess was ill in bed with a kidney complaint. The Princess had been on holiday in Denmark and was ill when she returned to Sweden. As a result, continued the Count, the Princess had telephoned Mr Douglas-

Home and asked him to put off his visit until she had recovered. They talked together, said the Count, for at least ten minutes. Asked if there had a quarrel he replied, 'I have not heard of any but possibly there was a lover's tiff. As far as the Swedish Court is concerned we are still expecting Mr Douglas-Home here when Princess Margaretha is better.' Then came a curious statement from Count Carl Reinhold von Essen, Master of Princess Sybilla's household: 'We think Mr Douglas-Home is a charming young man though not suited to marrying our Princess. The royal family is utterly democratic and wish it made clear that they have nothing whatsoever against Mr Douglas-Home's family.' At that the clan took umbrage and understood the statement to mean that Robin was not quite good enough for Swedish royalty. It was huffily pointed out that Robin Douglas-Home's family had produced distinguished noblemen long before the present Swedish dynasty was established.

When July and the time for his visit to Sweden came, Princess Margaretha was still bravely saying, 'I am ready to get engaged,' but there was a feeling that there had been a definite decision in Stockholm to withhold consent. Whatever really happened, it was suddenly all over. Speaking from the Hampshire home of his uncle, playwright William Douglas-Home, Robin announced tersely: 'For reasons which must remain private, I have decided not to visit Sweden in the foreseeable future.' Soon afterwards came a statement from the palace in Stockholm saying that Princess Margaretha, now twenty-four, was not yet ready for marriage.

There was no doubt of the unhappiness felt on both sides but Princess Margaretha put a brave face on things and carried on with her royal life. Robin took a plane to Nairobi where he decided to stay for a few months until he got over the break. At Nairobi airport the slim, fair-haired young man in grey flannels, tweed jacket and suede shoes was hurried to a waiting car without having to go through customs or passport formalities. He looked nervous and drawn. He was driven immediately to the home of his brother Charles, who was A.D.C. to the Governor of Kenya, Sir Evelyn Baring. By the end of the year he was in circulation again, a little sad but undoubtedly a figure of considerable interest, having come so near to marrying one of Europe's loveliest princesses.

Nine months after the romance ended he met Sandra Paul, one of the top models in London, tall, blonde, delicate and only eighteen. One of his friends said cynically, 'I'm not sure whether he actually loved her but when it came to women he always had to have the best.' He bought her an engagement ring of diamonds and rubies, asked her father, a Devon doctor, for her hand, and they were married in July 1959. But something went wrong. The marriage did not last.

Robin decided to take up piano playing again and once more could be seen in the smartest nightclubs, sitting at a white piano in his white dinner-jacket, fair hair gleaming, an ironic little smile on his lips. But times had changed. With the Sixties came the Beatles and the era of rock. His soft, romantic music sounded dated and he gave it up. He had a talent for writing and began to channel his creative ability into novels. Bitterly critical of his schooldays at Eton, he wrote a satirical novel, *Hot for Certain Ties*, showing his contempt for public-school education. It was published in 1964. He followed it with a strangely bitter story about a guitar player falling in love with a princess, which obviously had its roots in his own experience though he transferred the setting to the South Seas.

The beginning of 1967 saw an upsurge in his life. He was beginning to earn money with his pen and was very much in the social swing. He began to meet members of the old 'Margaret Set' and for a time, while Princess Margaret's marriage to Anthony Armstrong-Jones was going through a difficult patch, he started seeing her again. She obviously found solace in renewing her ties with old friends and Robin had been a favourite in the Fifties. They were seen around London, went to first nights, cocktail parties and to each other's homes. But as soon as Lord Snowdon arrived back in England from a trip to Japan, she thought it better not to see Robin and the friendship ended.

Many people thought that in a way Robin was always searching for Princess Margaretha again. He spent more and more time at his country house in Hampshire with his dogs and his aviary of budgerigars. He tried to write but friends felt that things were going wrong. He had escorted many beautiful women but as each liaison ended he felt greater despair. Once, in the final days of his depression, he asked a girl to marry him when they had only just met. He said that she reminded him of someone whom he had once been in love with. Not long afterwards, on 14 October 1968, he took his own life with an overdose of pills and alcohol. He was thirty-six years old. It was said of him that he was always chasing happiness and never quite succeeded in catching it. On his dressing-table he kept two photographs. One was of his wedding to Sandra Paul, the other of a smiling beauty signed, 'All my love, darling, Margaretha.' After his death a friend said, 'I think he really loved her. He never got over losing her.' And the beautiful princess? She married an Englishman, John Ambler, and came to live in the English shires.

# The Duke of York
## —AND—
# Lady Elizabeth Bowes Lyon

During the 1920 London season a fresh-faced Scottish girl with violet-blue eyes, soft brown hair and a sweet, merry smile became the toast of the town. Nineteen-year-old Lady Elizabeth Bowes Lyon, daughter of the Earl of Strathmore, was nothing like the cocktail-drinking, chain-smoking girls who came to be regarded as typical of that post-war era. She had, said Lady Airlie, lady-in-waiting to Queen Mary, a blend of radiant vitality, gaiety, kindness and sincerity. She avoided nightclubs and the smart set connected with the Prince of Wales but was usually seen at private balls in the splendid houses of her London friends, at Royal Ascot and country weekends. Everyone adored her.

Young men, many of them war heroes, swarmed around her but she remained elusive. She was as free as a lark and in no hurry to find a husband. When, therefore, she attended a ball at Lord Farquhar's house in Grosvenor Square one night in May 1920 and danced with the King's second son, Prince Albert, soon to be made Duke of York, she saw no reason to behave differently. Prince Albert, however, knew from the moment he first began to waltz with her that his life would never be the same again. 'He told me long afterwards that he had fallen in love that evening,' recorded Lady Airlie, 'although I do not think he realized it until much later.'

From that first waltz the shy, stammering Bertie, as he was known in the royal family, set himself to win Elizabeth Bowes Lyon and so began one of the most touching love stories of our times. Lady Elizabeth was not at all sure that she wanted to be royal. Coming from a warm family background with her roots in

149

the country, the thought of a lifetime in the public gaze filled her with horror. She did not accept the King's son until he had proposed three times. His tenacity paid off. Lady Elizabeth Bowes Lyon, destined to be Queen of England, became the most devoted and loving wife a man could have, helping her shy and diffident Bertie to achieve his full potential of greatness when he was thrust upon the throne after the abdication of his elder brother, Edward VIII.

Nothing could have been farther from her mind than marrying a future king as she grew up as the ninth child in a happy, gregarious family proud of its Scottish blood. Her father inherited the Earldom of Strathmore along with the much-haunted, turreted Glamis Castle, north of Dundee. The family also had houses in St James's Square, London, where she was born on 4 August 1900, and at St Paul's Waldenbury in Hertfordshire, where the carefree days of her Edwardian childhood seemed always to be golden.

As a baby she was said to have been 'a bundle of prettiness' and as a small girl quite enchanting with her soft brown hair, blue eyes and sweet face. Though her childhood was idyllic, she was never spoiled. Her father and her mother, Cecilia, who was the great-grand-daughter of the third Duke of Portland, believed in the old Victorian virtues without the stiffness. They were splendid parents with strong moral values, common sense and lack of snobbery. Lady Strathmore herself taught her youngest children to read and write as well as instructing them in the rudiments of music, dancing and drawing. They were also taught to be courteous to and interested in all kinds of people. There is a delightful record of a conversation the four-year-old Elizabeth had with the land agent at Glamis. As he waited to see Lord Strathmore she greeted him with, 'How do you do, Mr Ralston? I haven't seen you looking so well, not for years and years,' adding, as he struggled to hide his smile, 'I am sure you will be sorry to know that Lord Strathmore has got toothache.'

From earliest childhood Elizabeth became used to moving from one house to another with an army of nursemaids, footmen, ladies' maids, valet, butler, governess and pets. 'Home' was the warm, red-brick house at St Paul's Waldenbury, dripping with honeysuckle and roses, surrounded by magic woods and filled with pet animals of every kind. Elizabeth loved 'The Bury' and the hours she spent there with her brother David, born two years later and as close to her as a twin. Dressed in smocked pinafores and floppy sunhats the inseparable pair, called 'The Benjamins' by Lady Strathmore, played happily in woods and fields, their father having passed on to them his own love of the great outdoors. But as Elizabeth grew older it was Glamis with its dark, haunted passageways, its romantic towers and views of the far-off Grampian hills that caught her imagination. They spent the summer holidays there and she learned how to fish and how to appreciate the Scottish bagpipes. Lord Strathmore had the pipers march round the table three times every night after pudding had been served.

In spite of all this, the Bowes Lyons were not rich compared with some of Britain's oldest families. Their original fortune had been eroded by death duties and a certain lack of business acumen. Lady Strathmore was an excellent manager, however, and kept a strict eye on the housekeeping. The children's dresses were patched when necessary and they often had to make do. Lady Elizabeth, it was noted at one tennis party, had scuffed shoes and a racquet which had seen better days.

The family took up residence in St James's Square in May of each year and the children were taken to music and dancing classes, visited galleries and attended parties at friends' houses. Elizabeth and Bertie probably first encountered each other over the buns and crackers at one of these junior social events. Some royal observers believe it was at Lady Leicester's house.

As she grew older Elizabeth demonstrated a lively mind, sound intelligence and a great determination to see a job through once she had started it. Her excellent German governess Kathie Kuebler tutored her at home and saw her through her Junior Oxford Examinations, which were equivalent to the 'O' levels of today. At thirteen, according to Fraulein Kuebler, she had more maturity and understanding than her years warranted. She was a small, delicate figure with a pale complexion and beautiful eyes. Lady Strathmore's friends were already talking of how many hearts she would break.

Like thousands of others, her childhood came to an abrupt end with the outbreak of war in 1914. Four of her older brothers went immediately to join their regiments and Glamis was converted into a convalescent hospital for the wounded. Rows of beds filled the family drawing-room and lined the ancestral halls. While her elder sister Rose went to train as a nursing sister in London, fourteen-year-old Elizabeth became Lady Strathmore's right hand in the enormous job of running Glamis, receiving the maimed and shattered men sent back from the trenches, looking after them, trying to lift their spirits. Whenever she was not at her lessons, Lady Elizabeth was running errands, collecting mail from the post office, helping wounded men to write letters home, reading to the sightless. She played cards with them, joined in singing their favourite songs, made sure they were never short of tobacco or cigarettes. The soldiers came to look forward to seeing her slight, graceful figure moving between the beds. She made them feel she really cared about them.

The Strathmore family did not escape from the shadow of war. Elizabeth's brother Fergus, serving with the Black Watch, was killed at the Battle of Loos. Two years later her brother Michael was reported missing, believed killed. The strain and worry affected Lady Strathmore's health and for a time Elizabeth took her place. Happily, Michael was restored to them. By the time the war ended in 1918 more than 1,500 soldiers had passed through the castle. Lady Elizabeth had known them all by their Christian names, knew about their parents and what they did in civilian life. They had seen her grow from a schoolgirl into a beautiful young woman. Those who had been at Glamis never forgot her.

By the end of the war Elizabeth was eighteen, mature for her years after all she had experienced, but with a bubbling, unquenchable zest for life and fun. When society began to pick up the threads again in 1920 she entered into the London season with great enjoyment. She was seen in white lace at Ascot, in well-cut tweeds at Goodwood and she sparkled and shone at all the various balls and receptions being given in the capital's greatest houses. No wonder Prince Albert was enchanted as he waltzed with her at Lord Farquhar's. Good looking, honoured for his wartime bravery, he was only just beginning to emerge from a chrysalis of self-doubt and inadequacy. His own life and upbringing had been so different from hers.

The second son of King George V and Queen Mary was born on the wrong day to start with. Coming into the world on 14 December 1895 meant that he distracted attention from

Queen Victoria's annual day of mourning for her beloved Consort who had been dead for forty-four years. Only too aware of her displeasure, George, then Duke of York, more or less apologized to his grandmother for letting such a thing happen. She softened when George asked her to be godmother and said they had been thinking of calling the child Albert after the Prince Consort. 'I have a feeling that it might be a blessing for the dear little boy,' she wrote to his parents, 'and may be looked upon as a gift from God.' Little did she then realize that the 'dear little boy' would be crowned King exactly one hundred years after her own coronation.

Unlike Lady Elizabeth, Prince Albert did not grow up in a happy, relaxed family atmosphere. He was terrified of his father and was always in the shadow of his handsome, popular elder brother, the Prince of Wales. Though George V and Queen Mary no doubt had the best intentions, they had not the first notion of how to treat small children. George thought the best way to raise sons was to put the fear of God into them and Queen Mary, utterly devoid of the maternal instinct and hating the whole business of child-bearing, had no idea what to do at all. She failed to notice that Prince Albert had a sadistic nanny who neglected to feed him to such an extent that he developed stomach troubles. His tutor added to his distress by forcing him to change from writing with his left hand to the right. From that time on he developed a stammer which made it hard for him to express himself properly in English, let alone in French and German. He suffered from knock knees, too, and for a time was made to wear splints during the day and through the night as well, an experiment that caused him considerable pain. Small wonder that he was given to fits of temper and periods of gloom.

Prince Albert led a life remote from his contemporaries until he entered the naval college for junior cadets at Osborne on the Isle of Wight when he was thirteen. With his stammer and his diffident manner he was an easy target for bullying, but once away from the pressures of a royal upbringing his true, friendly nature began to emerge. He also discovered he had a considerable flair for athletics. The Navy suited him. He went on to the Royal Naval College at Dartmouth, became a midshipman in 1913 and, as he was only the King's second son, not heir to the throne, he was allowed to sign on for service with the wartime Navy. He distinguished himself at the Battle of Jutland and was mentioned in dispatches but to his dismay had to leave the Service at the end of 1917 for a serious operation for a duodenal ulcer, a legacy from his childhood.

When he had recovered from his illness he persuaded the King to let him join the Royal Naval Air Squadron. His confidence had increased considerably and, though he had no great love of flying, once he had made up his mind he became the first qualified pilot in the royal family. His father was pleased with him, considering that he had acquitted himself well. The next step was to send him to Trinity College, Cambridge, to readjust to civilian life and complete his formal education. He showed himself to be a diligent student with a real interest in the history of the Constitution.

As the Prince of Wales fell into deeper disfavour with his father because of his life-style, his affairs with married women and his love of night life – George V thought that anybody not in bed by 10.30 was up to no good – the King turned increasingly to his second son. Bertie was becoming popular in the country because of his interest in creating a better life for young people from underprivileged backgrounds. He was not a woman's man. He was, in fact, quite late turning his attention to the opposite sex. For a time he was seen around London with Grace Vanderbilt, daughter of Mrs Cornelia Vanderbilt, an American hostess of considerable wealth and ambition. But at twenty-five nothing had prepared him for the impact of a pair of deep-blue eyes belonging to the Lady Elizabeth Bowes Lyon.

Soon after their meeting at Lord Farquhar's the King decided to show his pleasure in what his second son had achieved and announced in the Birthday Honours List of 3 June 1920 that he had created him Duke of York. This gave Bertie fresh courage. From then on he set himself to win Lady Elizabeth, even though all the odds seemed against him. As far as he was concerned, no other girl existed.

Throughout the summer of 1920 Bertie took every chance that came his way to meet her. She was elusive, but they moved in more or less the same circles and Lady Elizabeth's friendship with his sister Princess Mary brought them together at times. Elizabeth liked Bertie immensely but treated him quite casually. When he called at the Strathmore's newly acquired London house in Bruton Street, to take her out to dinner or a dance, he would often find she was not ready. He would chat to Lord and Lady Strathmore, who were beginning to feel a bit sorry for him. Elizabeth's mother found him sensitive and charming but was not at all impressed by the fact that he was royal. Lord Strathmore considered him a thoroughly nice young chap.

Strangely enough, considering her supposed lack of maternal feeling, it was Queen Mary who first noticed her son's growing love for Lady Elizabeth. She had heard that Lloyd George had told the King that the country would not tolerate a foreign alliance for the Prince of Wales and that the Duke of York should also look for a bride among the English aristocracy. Queen Mary confided to her friend, Lady Airlie, 'I don't think Bertie will be sorry to hear that. I have discovered that he is very much attracted to Lady Elizabeth Bowes Lyon. He's always talking about her.'

The Strathmores, as usual, took their summer holidays at Glamis and Lady Elizabeth went with them. By chance, or perhaps with Queen Mary's words at the back of her mind, Lady Airlie invited Princess Mary and the Duke of York to stay at her own Scottish home, Cortachy Castle. Lord Strathmore, who loved the company of young people and was a genial host, invited them all to Glamis. Elizabeth noticed how relaxed Bertie was, how he hardly stuttered at all and how he laughed at her teasing, gentle wit. The Duke had fresh achievements to lay at her feet. He had won the R.A.F. Doubles at Wimbledon with his friend Dr Louis Greig, proving himself a brilliant tennis player of professional standard, and he had made his first appearance in the House of Lords. The three young people had a wonderful time together. Bertie fell just a bit more in love when he saw Elizabeth dressed in rose-pink brocade with pearls in her hair for a ball at Glamis.

Back in London at the end of autumn Lady Elizabeth continued to visit her friend Princess Mary at Buckingham Palace. On one of these visits she met Queen Mary privately and came under her shrewd gaze. Bertie's mother obviously liked what she saw but, convinced that mothers should not meddle in their children's love affairs, said nothing.

By the spring of 1921 the relationship was causing great interest and the Duke of York told his parents that he intended to ask Lady Elizabeth to marry him. 'You will be a lucky fellow if she accepts you,' said George V, who thought her a peach and streets ahead of most modern girls with their cigarette holders and flighty ways.

Bertie proposed but was gently and firmly refused. Elizabeth was not at all happy at the prospect of becoming a member of the royal family. She realized how restricted her life would become. It is strange that one who has been so much loved by the public and who has shown such genius for sharing her humanity with masses of people should fear public life most of all. There was no idea at this time, of course, that Bertie would have to wear the Crown. Lady Strathmore herself made a profound remark after the refusal. 'I do hope he will find a nice wife who will make him happy. I like him so much and he is a man who will be made or marred by his wife.'

They continued to see each other. Lady Elizabeth was sad but convinced she had done the right thing. Bertie's proposal was by no means the only one she turned down that year. That summer Lady Strathmore was very ill and Elizabeth went to Scotland to look after her. Bertie stayed with Lady Airlie again and was invited to Glamis for the pheasant shooting. 'It is delightful here,' he wrote to his mother. 'Elizabeth is very kind to me. The more I see her, the more I like her.' Queen Mary also arrived in Scotland *en route* for Balmoral and decided to invite herself to Glamis for tea so that she could review the situation. Over rich fruit cake and scones she studied her young hostess. 'She is the one girl who could make Bertie happy,' she admitted later, 'but I shall say nothing to either of them.'

Lady Airlie, like the Queen, was deeply disappointed when Lady Elizabeth refused the Duke of York. Both young people knew she was sympathetic towards them and she became their confidante. They called separately at her flat to unburden themselves. Bertie, she said, could talk of nothing but Elizabeth. He was no Lothario but he was so deeply in love his humility was quite touching.

Princess Mary, engaged to Viscount Lascelles, was to be married at Westminster Abbey the following February and it was only natural that she should ask her dear friend Lady Elizabeth to be one of her eight bridesmaids. It was the first post-war royal wedding and it was to be accorded the status of a State cere-monial. When the day arrived the whole of London was in a festive mood and for the first time Elizabeth rode in state through cheering crowds. She looked exquisite in a dress made from cloth of silver with a huge silver rose at the hip and a coronet of silver leaves in her dark hair. It did not go unnoticed that the Duke of York hardly took his eyes off her. They sat together at the reception and when the guests rushed down to the forecourt of Buckingham Palace to see Princess Mary and her husband leave for their honeymoon, they stood together, a little apart from the others.

But after the wedding Elizabeth was snatched away to Paris. Another bridesmaid, Diamond Hardinge, whose father was British Ambassador, invited her to stay at the Embassy in the Rue de Faubourg St Honoré. It was the start of a life-long love affair with France. She had a wonderful time and any number of handsome young attachés were anxious to escort her to the cafés, to balls and to picnics at Fontainebleau. One of her Embassy admirers was said to have proposed to her but she did not take any of them seriously.

When she returned to England that September Bertie was again invited to Glamis and Lady Elizabeth once more proved a most delightful hostess. For the second time he proposed and for the second time she sadly and gently declined his offer. His only consolation was that he knew she was turning down other offers as well. And she *had* assured him that she was very fond of him.

That winter of 1922 Lady Elizabeth's family noticed a change in her. She seemed pre-occupied, concerned and somewhat confused about her emotions. Lady Strathmore wrote: 'That winter was the first time I have ever known Elizabeth really worried. I think she was torn between her longing to make Bertie happy and her reluctance to take on the big responsibilities which this marriage must bring.'

The two of them were frequently together at St Paul's Walden-bury. They would go for long country walks, Elizabeth dressed in a tweed suit, long woolly scarf and pull-on hat. Bertie was asked to spend a weekend at 'The Bury' on Saturday, 13 January 1923. He must have made up his mind to have one final attempt at making Elizabeth change her mind and to have confided his intentions to his parents before travelling down to Hertfordshire. They had, it appears, arranged a code so that he could send a message to signal his success or failure.

On the Sunday morning of that weekend the young couple went for a walk through Elizabeth's favourite wood at 'The Bury', one in which she had played happily as a child with her brother

David. There the young Duke stammered out his proposal for the third time. To his intense joy Elizabeth looked up into his anxious face and answered, 'Oh, Bertie, yes.' They said afterwards that neither knew who was the more surprised. Hand-in-hand, laughing, they rushed back to the house to give their good news to Lord and Lady Strathmore. The Duke immediately sent a telegram to the King and Queen which simply said, 'All right. Bertie.'

The following day Bertie went to Sandringham. King George noted in his diary, 'Bertie, with Greig, arrived after tea and informed us that he was engaged to Elizabeth Bowes Lyon to which we gladly gave our consent. I trust they will be very happy.' Lady Airlie, who had been as eager as anyone for the match, sent a note of congratulation and the Duke replied to her in a letter which did not try to conceal his overflowing emotions: 'How can I thank you enough for your charming letter to me about the wonderful happening in my life which has come to pass, and my dream, which has at last been realized. It seems too marvellous to me that my darling Elizabeth will one day be my wife.... '

The engagement was announced in a Court Circular from Sandringham on 16 January and the Strathmore's Bruton Street house was besieged by reporters and photographers. Lady Elizabeth was seen to be wearing a beautiful engagement ring, a large Kashmir sapphire with diamonds.

Four days after the announcement the Duke took Lady Elizabeth and her parents to meet the King and Queen. If she was slightly nervous, Lord and Lady Strathmore showed no signs of being awed by the situation. As Peter Lane comments in his biography of the Queen Mother, 'Their families had been intimate with kings and queens long before the Hanoverians were brought to the throne of Great Britain and Ireland.' There was certainly nothing intimidating about the royal dwelling. At that time Their Majesties lived in what Harold Nicolson called 'a glum little villa' called York Cottage while the old Queen Alexandra lived at the big house on the Sandringham estate. Lady Strathmore said the drawing-room reminded her of a room in her father-in-law's old house in Belgrave Mansions. But almost at once a bond was formed between Lady Elizabeth and the King. He thoroughly approved of her, forgot to play the martinet and treated her in a kind and fatherly manner.

Most endearing of all, she seemed to understand his rather odd sense of humour. 'She is a pretty and charming girl,' he recorded in his diary after the visit. 'Bertie is a very lucky fellow.'

The wedding was looked forward to with great excitement. For one thing it was considered quite revolutionary that the King's son should be marrying a commoner. With a few notable exceptions, the practice of royal princes choosing their brides from great landowning families had almost died out by the end of the fifteenth century. They began to marry princesses from foreign courts in order to keep the blood royal, often with lamentable results. Marriages between royalty and commoner were creeping back but none had been as close to the throne as Bertie and Elizabeth. Westminster Abbey was chosen for the ceremony. It would be the first time a king's son had been married there since 1382 when Richard II married Anne of Bohemia.

The morning of 26 April 1923 turned out to be cool and drizzly but George V was certain that the sun came out as Lady Elizabeth entered the Abbey. She was a delicate, medieval figure in a dress of ivory-coloured chiffon moire with a square neck, a panel of silver lace from neck to hem and trailing sleeves of Nottingham lace. Her veil, prettily draped about her head, left her face uncovered. The *Daily Mirror* that day reported: 'Such a sweet, composed little bride – she looked almost ethereal, just a trail of white and silver as she passed into the dim vastness of the Abbey, attended by her maids who surrounded her like a sea mist, all white and green, with white flowers in their hair.' She went into the Abbey on the arm of her father Lord Strathmore, resplendent in his scarlet uniform as Lord Lieutenant of Forfar, pausing for a moment to lay her bouquet of white York roses on the tomb of the unknown warrior. So typical of her, said the papers next day, that in the moment of her greatest happiness she should remember her brother Fergus and all those who died with him. She emerged an hour later smiling radiantly on the arm of the happiest R.A.F. officer in the country, handsome in full-dress uniform, wonderfully proud of Her Royal Highness, now the third lady in the land. Obviously relieved that the great pageantry in the Abbey was over, they drove back to Buckingham Palace in the Glass Coach through tumultuous crowds, including loudly vocal Scottish contingents. When they made the now traditional appearance on the palace balcony the crowds streamed down

159

The Mall. 'There was a sea of waving handkerchiefs,' Elizabeth remembered, 'everyone was so happy.'

There was a huge wedding breakfast with eight courses and a giant wedding cake nine feet high which weighed eight hundred pounds and had real gold tokens in the first huge slice. When the couple left for their honeymoon Elizabeth took with her a trousseau which had been lovingly stitched by a lady at Glamis who had been sewing for the Strathmores all her life. The new Duchess of York was not the sort of person to suddenly switch loyalties. The same thoughtfulness had made her use Nottingham lace for part of her wedding dress 'because the industry is in such difficulties'. She looked delightful in her simple going-away outfit of soft mushroom silk with a matching cloche hat and a string of pearls and seemed to enjoy the good-natured public acclaim as she and the Duke laughed and waved all the way to Waterloo Station. The Prince of Wales, only too conscious that people were beginning to ask when he was going to find himself a suitable bride, saw them off on the station platform as they travelled to their first-night destination in Surrey in a compartment filled with white roses, carnations and lilies-of-the-valley. The journey took thirty-five minutes and there were people waving and cheering along every inch of the track.

The Duke and Duchess had been invited to spend the first part of their honeymoon at Mrs Ronnie Greville's Regency house Polesden Lacey, set in pine trees and beautiful gardens in the Surrey hills. Then they moved on to Glamis where Lady Strathmore had prepared a trio of rooms specially for them. Unfortunately the weather was appalling and to her utter dismay Elizabeth caught whooping-cough and was confined to bed. Her sense of humour came to the rescue and while writing to Queen Mary that the whole thing was 'not very romantic' she enjoyed being spoiled by her new husband as she sat propped up by pillows in one of the great Strathmore fourposters.

Their first home was to be White Lodge in Richmond Park, one of the royal Grace and Favour houses, built in 1727 by King George II as 'a place of refreshment after the chase'. It was a tall, rambling house, somewhat chilly, but Queen Mary had it redecorated, electricity installed and other modern conveniences completed before their return. The furniture was rather large and gloomy and the kitchens bleak and institutional, but the

Duchess of York, with her exquisite tact, thanked Queen Mary for all she had done and described her home as 'airy'. It was certainly set in beautiful surroundings. When Elizabeth invited her in-laws for lunch for the first time she warned them, with the nervousness of a new bride, that the cooking would be very plain as their kitchen staff was not up to palace standards. She advised her cook not to try anything too ambitious for dessert. Good stewed fruit and custard would be suitable! The lunch was a success. Queen Mary noticed how different the house looked from the days when she knew it. Elizabeth had given it her own special touch, bowls of sweet-smelling flowers in every corner, the beautiful wedding presents they had received displayed to greatest advantage. It was a real home.

The Duke and Duchess were sociable, enjoyed dancing, the company of friends and the occasional visit to the cinema at Marble Arch, which they made incognito to avoid fuss. But they were at their happiest alone together in the evenings when the Duke would work at his *petit point* embroidery, which, like the Prince of Wales, he had learned from Queen Mary, and the Duchess would play the piano to him or sit quietly reading. Sir John Wheeler-Bennett, who became George VI's official biographer, summed it up when he wrote that 'from the first days of his marriage his home life was his refuge and safeguard against the world and on the love and companionship of his wife was based his life long contentment'. For the first time in his life someone really believed in him.

But the Yorks did not have a great deal of time to spend in their new home. Every post brought a shoal of requests and their duties became more demanding every day. The obvious happiness of the young couple endeared them to the public and the royal family quickly realized that they had indeed found a winner in 'the smiling Duchess'. Their first appearance in public together was at the Royal Air Force pageant at Hendon at the end of June. The close bond between the two was soon noticed as she took her place beside him on public platforms and whenever he had to speak. Sometimes he would just glance towards her and she would give him an encouraging look. At others she could be seen to be mouthing the words he had to say 'as if by the hypnotism of love she was calling the sounds from his throat', wrote David Duff in his biography *Elizabeth of Glamis*.

Sometimes her hand would steal out to touch his. It was as though they had decided to conquer the problem of his speech impediment together.

They went on a five-month trip to Africa in December 1924, sleeping in tents under star-studded skies and travelling down the Nile by paddle-steamer. It was like a second honeymoon. Their joy was increased the following year when Elizabeth announced that she was pregnant and on Wednesday, 21 April 1926 gave birth to a fine baby daughter, Princess Elizabeth, who would one day be Queen of England. Four years later, when she found she was pregnant again, she decided she would like this baby to be Scottish by birth and moved home to Glamis. On 21 August 1930 Princess Margaret came into the world, the first member of the royal family to be born in Scotland since 1602. The Scottish people were delighted, especially those in the neighbourhood of Glamis.

The Duke and Duchess of York with their two lively, impish young daughters became the pattern of ideal family life for Britain in the following years. They were wonderfully happy, and with help from a remarkable Australian speech therapist called Lionel Logue Bertie was beginning to conquer the impediment in his speech. He lost his fears about speaking in public and gradually managed to get through a speech without the painful pauses which had so embarrassed both him and his audience. Then came the great blow: the Abdication.

George V had died peacefully at Sandringham on 20 January 1936 and the Prince of Wales had come to the throne as King Edward VIII. But all that year the storm clouds were gathering as it became clear that the popular young King was only prepared to stay on one condition. He was deeply in love with and wished to marry Mrs Wallis Simpson, an American divorcee, who was totally unacceptable to the British government and the royal family. Queen Mary angrily reminded him of 'his duty'. The Yorks felt sick at heart as they saw their whole way of life threatened. Bertie, next in line, protested that he had not been trained to be King like his brother and had never even *seen* a State paper.

Protestations, calls to duty, were in vain. Edward felt he could not bear the burden of kingship without the woman he loved and on Thursday, 10 December 1936 signed the Instrument of

Abdication, and the Abdication Bill was rushed through the Houses of Parliament on the following day. Bertie broke down and wept when he knew that there was no escape from his destiny and Elizabeth, weak with influenza, also wept when she discovered she was Queen. Her first visitor was her mother-in-law, who curtsied to her as she lay on her sickbed.

Yet these two, who so reluctantly came to the throne of England, were to become loved and cherished by the British people as they became a symbol of stability, faith and family life in the terrible years ahead. Elizabeth, when she had recovered, turned to her husband and said, 'We can do it, Bertie.' Queen Mary had no doubt about it. 'The Yorks will do it very well,' she told everyone.

On 12 May 1937 they drove in the Gold Coach from Buckingham Palace to Westminster Abbey for the Coronation. As the great, glittering crown was placed on his head George VI, as he had become, seemed to be in a trance. His Queen, exquisite in her Coronation robes, was seen to pray fervently.

Within a year any doubts that anyone might have had about whether they could cope were firmly dispelled. Archbishop Lang wrote to them about the impression he had from among all kinds of people with regard to their King and Queen. 'At first the feeling was one of sympathy and hope. It has now become a feeling of confidence and admiration.'

In the summer of 1937 they made a happy, memorable tour of Canada and America but were aware all the time of storm clouds gathering over Europe. Their impact on the New World was astonishing. One senator told the King, 'You're a great Queen picker,' and in Canada, after a rapturous reception everywhere, the King was told there was no question of Canada being isolationist if war should ever come – 'not after this visit'.

When war did come in September 1939 the King and Queen made one of the greatest decisions of their lives – to stay in London with their people and face the dangers with them. Night after night the German bombers came and the following morning the small, neat figures of Bertie and Elizabeth could be seen making their way through the ravaged streets of the capital to give sympathy and moral support. In the badly hit East End Elizabeth offered to hold the baby of a young woman in some difficulty. As she stood there smiling down at the bundle in her arms a Cockney voice called out, 'Ain't she just bloody lovely.' Another day, as Bertie stood talking to a group of weary rescue workers, the ruins around them still smouldering, a workman cried out, 'Thank God for a good King,' and with infinite grace he replied, 'Thank God for a good people.' Bombs fell on the Palace too, much to Elizabeth's relief for then, she said, she could 'look the East End in the face'. Their war effort never faltered. While the King was away visiting the troops the Queen visited badly bombed towns in other parts of the country, hospitals, dockyards and airfields. When she was old enough Princess Elizabeth joined the A.T.S. and went on to become something of an expert at tinkering with lorries.

With the end of the war it became obvious that they had been gloriously successful. Huge cheering crowds surrounded them wherever they went. It was felt that no King and Queen could have given their country better moral support than they had through those dark years. The King wrote to his mother that they were dumbfounded by the acclaim of the people and the letters that had poured in to them from all over the world.

Normal life resumed for most people but those closest to him slowly began to realize that the King was paying a price for his mighty effort. He was among the war wounded, and beginning to feel 'an awful reaction'. He desperately wanted to be left alone for a while with his family and to be allowed to raise his South Downs sheep and Red Poll cattle. He knew in his heart this was not possible but he loved and understood the countryside and country matters and was always happy when he was close to the soil. His favourite sport was shooting and he would go out in all weathers. Once, after wild-fowling in Norfolk, he recorded in his game book, 'Snow and a very cold east wind. I spent four hours in a hide in a kale field.' His greatest energy, however, went into the development and management of the royal estates at Sandringham and Balmoral where, after fulfilling demanding State duties, he relaxed more than anywhere else and threw himself into the role of country landowner and farmer. Very little went on that he was not aware of. He was interested in every detail of day-to-day farming as well as being concerned for the welfare of his tenants and anxious to carry out any improvements he felt necessary to their estate cottages. Wearing tweeds and carrying a stout stick, he would stride purposefully about his acres, sometimes accompanied by the Queen wearing a head-scarf and no-nonsense shoes. He was especially fond of pigs.

The next few years brought events that gave them both immense pleasure. They enjoyed a memorable tour of South Africa and had the joy of seeing Princess Elizabeth happily married to Prince Philip. The King wrote to his beloved daughter, 'Your leaving us has left a great blank in our lives but do remember that your old house is still yours and do come back to it as much and as often as possible. I can see that you are sublimely happy with Philip, which is right, but don't forget us, is the wish of your ever loving and devoted papa.'

The King and Queen celebrated their own Silver Wedding in April 1948 and George confessed that he was both amazed and proud at the public's affectionate and whole-hearted response to the anniversary. Thousands of letters were delivered to Buckingham Palace reflecting the admiration and love felt by ordinary people.

The Queen, however, could not disguise the fact that she was worried about the King's health. He had lost a great deal of weight on the South Africa trip and had been complaining of agonizing cramp in the legs. While taking medicine to relieve the pain, he insisted on carrying out all his duties, including playing a full part in a State visit by the King and Queen of Denmark. By November, however, his doctors diagnosed that he was suffering from arteriosclerosis and warned that gangrene might set in. While he was lying seriously ill in one part of the palace, his grandson Prince Charles was born in another wing. The doctors' treatment worked so well that he was able to attend the christening and to go to Sandringham with his family that Christmas. Throughout the next year there seemed to be a steady improvement in his health and *The Times* wrote, 'It would be impossible to over estimate the reinforcement the King has derived from the serene and steady support of the Queen....'

It was not until 1951, when he was ordered to bed with influenza and the Queen had to act as host to the King of Norway on a State visit, that the first real danger signals were seen. He recovered enough to go with the family to Balmoral in August but while there caught another chill. This time the doctors advised him to return to London so that a sample of tissue could be taken from the lung. The results were serious. By September he was told that he had to have a lung removed because of a blockage in one of the bronchial tubes. The Queen was told that he had cancer, a fact that she vowed she would keep from him as long as possible. To her horror she learned that, even if he took life easily, Bertie had only a few more years to live.

The reality was much harsher. On the last day of the year Princess Elizabeth and Prince Philip were due to fly to East Africa on the first stage of their trip to Australia. The King insisted that he wanted to go with the Queen to the airport to see them off. He stood on the roof of the building waving until the plane was a mere speck in the sky, his face gaunt, his silver-streaked hair dishevelled in the wind. It was the last picture of him ever taken.

His last days were spent at Sandringham and they were happy ones. He was able to go out shooting with his friends and local farmers and to enjoy the company of his little grandchildren Prince Charles and Princess Anne. On the night of 5 February he said a prayer with them before kissing them both goodnight, dined with his wife and Princess Margaret and went quietly to bed in the ground-floor room he had used ever since his illness. During the night, he died. The love story of Bertie and Elizabeth was over. Or was it?

Elizabeth was only fifty-one when she was widowed. The strain imposed on her by the last months of the King's illness had left its mark. She had lost a stone in weight, her eyes betrayed great sadness and some people wondered if she would ever again greet them with the radiance that had originally won her the title of 'The Smiling Duchess'. She knew that Bertie would have wanted her to keep going so, on the day after his death, she left the quiet sanctuary of her own rooms and went downstairs to play games with her grandchildren. 'I've got to start sometime and it is better now than later,' she explained. Making her first appearance in public was more difficult but Winston Churchill, who referred to her as 'that valiant woman', convinced her that she was needed.

After a period of grief, the depth of which only she can know, the Queen Mother, as she has been known ever since, emerged to begin all over again. She was Colonel-in-Chief of several regiments and it was always her practice to wish them God speed when they left for service overseas. When she heard the First Battalion of the Black Watch had been ordered to Korea she flew from Windsor to Fife to see them off. Dressed in black with a brooch of diamonds, she was taking the first courageous steps into the future. When she drove from Clarence House to attend the Coronation at Westminster the deep sympathy for her was almost tangible but she was already back in harness 'glittering from top to toe, diamonds everywhere'. Head erect, she watched her daughter being crowned.

In a letter in which she thanked people for their kindness and tributes she referred to Bertie as 'my dear husband, a great and noble King', and said that she had only one wish and that was 'to be allowed to continue the work that we sought to do together'. She has more than triumphed in that as the world well knows.

# Juan Carlos of Spain
## —AND—
## Princess Sophia

When General Franco died in 1975 and Juan Carlos became King of Spain he gave a new look to a country that had lived for a long time under a fascist dictator. He turned it into a democracy. In the years that followed the world suddenly seemed to be full of handsome Spaniards. There was Severiano Ballesteros playing golf, Julio Iglesias singing love songs, Placido Domingo singing opera, Espartaco, a new heart-throb in the bullring. And at the Zarzuela Palace outside Madrid there was Juan Carlos himself, six feet tall, athletic, good-looking, and with a pretty, talented Queen. Together they seemed to have given a completely fresh outlook to all things Spanish. Many Spaniards say, with a twinkle in their eyes, that it was because Juan Carlos fell in love with the right girl that the return of the monarchy after an absence of forty-four years is so successful today.

They met in England at the wedding of the Duke of Kent and Katherine Worsley. Truly met, that is. They had encountered each other before but this was the first significant meeting. Prince Juan Carlos, as he was then known, was assigned to be official escort of Princess Sophia of Greece. 'For once,' said Sophia later, 'protocol turned up trumps.'

Elderly, watchful relatives noticed that at all the parties after the wedding they seemed to be inseparable. They also spent hours chatting over cups of tea at the Savoy. Sophia's brother Crown Prince Constantine rang his parents in Athens and said they should prepare themselves for a surprise: Juan Carlos was at the wedding and he was paying an awful lot of attention to their daughter, adding, 'Not that she seemed to mind.'

Juan Carlos and Sophia are distant cousins. When they ran into each other before, usually at royal family occasions, they were either too young or too occupied to notice. Juan Carlos was for many years a prince-in-waiting, waiting for a throne that might never be his. King Alfonso XIII, his grandfather, had been thrown out of Spain because he was not very good at kingship and spent too much time with the ladies. His father, Don Juan, was therefore forced to live in exile as pretender to the throne while Spain became first a republic, then a dictatorship. Prince Juan Carlos was born in Rome on 5 January 1938 and baptized by Cardinal Eugenio Pacelli, who was to become Pope Pius XII. As a boy he knew what it was to be rootless. From 1942 until 1946 he lived with his parents in Lausanne where he began his education. Then they moved on to Estoril in Portugal. But in 1947 came a decision that changed his life.

General Franco, who had ruled Spain since the end of the Spanish Civil War, announced in 1947 that after he died Spain would once more become a kingdom. There were talks with Don Juan and he agreed that it would be better for him to stand down and for his son to be named as Franco's successor. From the age of fifteen the Prince lived in Spain being carefully groomed by Franco for the throne. Once the old dictator declared, 'I love him as if he were my own son.'

By the time he was ready for the Saragossa Military Academy Juan Carlos was a splendid young man and romantically good looking, much more Spanish in appearance than his father in spite of his fair, wavy hair. His education had increased his confidence. When cadets began to address him as 'Your Highness' he replied, 'Drop that,' and told them to call him Juanito. When he entered the Acadamy in December 1955 at the age of seventeen, cadets had to go through a ceremony in which they kissed the red and gold flag of Spain. A large monarchist crowd had gathered, and when it came to Juanito's turn up went a tremendous shout: 'Long live the King.'

The next few years were spent training at the Naval Academy, learning to fly, studying at the University of Madrid and gaining first-hand experience of various ministries. Women fell for him like ninepins but he was not a ladies' man. The only two names linked with his before he met Princess Sophia were those of Maria Gabriella, daughter of King Umberto of Italy, and Princess Isabelle, daughter of the Count of Paris, who was older than he.

By the time he attended the Kent wedding in England in 1961 he was a young man of considerable presence, and as far as he was concerned Princess Sophia, daughter of King Paul and Queen Frederika of Greece, was different from any other royal princess he had ever met. She was serious, yet full of fun; clever, but always wanting to learn more. Above all she was compassionate and kind, a quality which endeared her to everyone.

Princess Sophia was born into the Greek royal family on 2 November 1938 at Psychico, just outside Athens. A twenty-one-gun salute celebrated her arrival. When war broke out she had to escape from Greece with her family and spent five years abroad, most of the time in South Africa. Returning home, she went to a country school with girls drawn from all classes of Greek life. She was shy and for a time had to wear a brace on her teeth. In spite of this, and the fact that she was happy being back in her own country, she was sent abroad at thirteen to be subjected to the firm discipline of one of the Kurt Hahn schools in Germany – Schloss Salem, which was a co-educational fore-runner of Gordonstoun in Scotland. Once she got over her homesickness she enjoyed it.

She returned to Greece when she was eighteen and enrolled at a nursing school, obtained her diploma and became a fully-trained childrens' nurse. Her mother had founded an orphanage in Athens and Sophia worked there, undertaking all the day and night duties required of her. Queen Frederika, who had a passion for learning, felt that her daughters Sophia and Irène had still not been educated enough. She hired a Greek professor who taught them ancient Greek, literature, history, art and archae-ology. Princess Sophia emerged from it all without a hint of being a blue-stocking. She had grown up into a strikingly attrac-tive girl with a delightful pixie-ish smile.

She first encountered Juan Carlos on a romantic cruise organ-ized for members of European royal families by Queen Frederika, but she was only fifteen and he was sixteen. They hardly noticed each other. The second time was at the Olympic Games in Italy six years later when all the attention was on Crown Prince Constantine, who won a gold medal. The third time, at the Duke of Kent's wedding, was a different matter. Juan Carlos could not take his eyes off the pretty Greek princess with her vivacious personality. They waltzed together time after time and he fell completely in love. Once he had decided that he could not live without her, the courtship was swift and decisive.

After the wedding Juan Carlos and his parents were asked to spend a holiday at the Greek royal family's summer residence on the island of Corfu. During the hot days they sailed and swam, and at night sat under the stars. In Corfu they well and truly fell in love. The following winter the Prince was asked to join Sophia's family again on a holiday in a Swiss ski resort. One day they were left alone. The Princess told a close friend later, 'He gave me a bracelet and said, "We'll get married, eh?"' It was the forthright proposal of a man of action. Sophia did not hesitate. She knew this was the man for her. When her father King Paul was told the news and asked for her hand in marriage, he was so delighted that he threw his arms around one of his courtiers and hugged him.

Princess Sophia's mother wrote in her autobiography, 'We were delighted as Juanito, as we call him in the family, is incredibly good looking. He has fair, curly hair which he personally dislikes, but all elderly ladies, like myself, simply adore. He has dark eyes with long lashes, is tall and athletic and turns his charm on and off as he likes! But what is more important, he is intelligent, has modern ideas and is kind and gentle. He has enough pride to be a real Spaniard, but also enough loving understanding to be able to easily forgive other people's transgressions.'

As Juan Carlos was Catholic and Princess Sophia Greek Orthodox there had to be long discussions before they married. Sophia did not want to change her religion immediately. It was agreed that there should be two ceremonies. The wedding was eventually fixed for 14 May 1962.

Athens was a riot of colour for the occasion and the sun shone with the first real heat of the summer. Princess Sophia drove first to the Catholic church, which had been filled with red and yellow carnations, the national colours of Spain, in a blue-and-gold bridal coach drawn by six white horses. King Paul sat proudly by her side and her brother Constantine, in full-dress uniform complete with sword, rode on horseback by the side of the carriage. She was a lovely bride, all in white lace, with her mother's lace wedding veil over her tiara. Her long train was carried by six bridesmaids, among them Princess Alexandra of Kent. The second ceremony, in the Greek Orthodox Cathedral, was wonderfully ornate and the ritual gold crowns were passed over the heads of the bride and bridegroom three times as showers of rose petals fell from the ceiling above.

Presents poured into the palace in Athens, including a fine diamond pin from Franco for the bride. But there was one present which Princess Sophia said she would treasure more than anything. When asked what she would like to be given for a wedding present by the Greek Agricultural Workers' Union she said, 'I only want the seedling of a laurel tree. I will let it grow, then wherever I live I shall plant it in my garden to remind me of my country.' The laurel tree went with her to Spain.

After their wedding Juan Carlos was still waiting in the political wings to see if he would ever really become King. Seven years later came affirmation of all his hopes and dreams. In 1969 General Franco formally named Juan Carlos as his successor and the Prince took his oath as the future King of Spain. It was an emotional moment for all around him and especially for Princess Sophia, now mother of three children, who had to accustom herself to the idea of being Queen.

From that day on Juan Carlos was always present in the background whenever Franco appeared in public. Though Princess Sophia accompanied him on several important visits overseas, she continued to behave like an ordinary mother at home, collecting her children from school, supervising their meals. Their happy and contented family life with their children – Doña Elena, born in 1963, Doña Cristina, born in 1965, and Don Felipe, now Prince of the Asturias, born in 1968 – was evident to everyone who saw them. So was the fact that they were still in love.

Their moment of destiny came in 1975 when General Franco died and Juan Carlos became King, bringing the monarchy back to Spain at last.

At his proclamation he wore the uniform of the Supreme Commander of the armed forces. Sophia, now to be known as Queen Sophia, wore a simple pink dress. The ceremonial robes and jewels were left in a display cabinet at Aranjuez Castle. Juan Carlos had decided that simplicity was to be the keynote of his monarchy. He assumed power with the minimum of trouble mainly due to the respect in which he was held.

Two days after being invested as Queen thirty-seven-year-old Sophia, still slim and attractive in an amazingly youthful way, was back at her regular Saturday morning course at Madrid University, mixing with students and talking to them in her friendly, informal manner. They adore her. Juan Carlos was always sure that the Spaniards would take her to their hearts, and he was right.

She is quickly on the scene of any disaster. When a collision in Salamanca between a train and a school bus killed twenty-eight children just before Christmas in 1978, she was there among the grieving relatives before they realized who she was. Simply dressed, her face composed but sad, she put her arm around one mother's shoulders. 'The least I could do was come to see you.' Someone said to her, 'You can understand, you have children.'

Juan Carlos watches her with tenderness in his eyes. They have a marvellous working partnership. Their faith and trust in each other was never more necessary than on the night of 23 February 1981. It was the night on which the democracy that Juan Carlos had so carefully nurtured since he became King nearly perished. Without warning two hundred members of the para-military *Guardia Civil*, under the command of Colonel Tejero, stormed into Parliament while it was in session, firing automatic weapons and smashing the TV cameras set up to record the proceedings. But they overlooked one. The whole terrifying assault was seen by the Spanish people and by the King, who was in his office at the time. He learned that certain generals in the Army with right-wing sympathies had masterminded the coup to 'save' Spain from democratic government. Juan Carlos calmly picked up the telephone and spoke to every general he could reach, telling them he did not support the coup and ordering them to be loyal to the constitution. He then summoned a television crew to the palace, hastily changed out of the sports clothes he was wearing into his uniform as commander-in-chief, and spoke directly to the Spanish people, commanding the Army to obey him. His quick thinking and courage saved Spain from another military dictatorship.

All the time this was going on Queen Sophia and his children were waiting quietly in another room, wondering how the night would end. Speaking to *Sunday Times* reporter Susan Crosland, Juan Carlos said, 'The worst thing is to show fear,' though security around his family, he admitted , was pretty right. 'The children don't like it, but it's necessary.'

They refused to move into the enormous royal palace in the heart of Madrid, saying they would feel like tourists in a museum. Instead they choose to live at Zarzuela, a two-storey brick house set in woodlands north of Madrid which used to be a seventeenth-century hunting lodge. They have declined a retinue of servants and the King has resisted all attempts to make court life a rich and privileged affair.

They are modern, love being with their children, wear slacks and sweaters when they are off duty and have given the country a new feeling of youth and buoyancy. There is no more attractive sight in Spain than Queen Sophia in trousers and T-shirt riding on the back of the King's motorbike. If the monarchy in Spain is a success story, the answer lies in the courage of Juan Carlos and Queen Sophia's love for him, which he knows will back him all the way.

# Shah of Iran
## —AND—
# Farah Diba

Ever since she was a child Farah Diba had been taught to regard His Imperial Majesty Mohammed Reza Shah Pahlavi with reverence and awe. Not only was he the ruler of her country, the ancient kingdom of Persia now called Iran, but he was the King of Kings, Allah's Shadow on Earth, an almost mythical being under divine protection.

That he was also a man with human emotions, desperately in need of love and affection, was something that would never have occurred to the slender, dark-eyed, nineteen-year-old student until she came face to face with him one evening in May 1958 and noticed the sadness in his eyes.

Farah was only three years old when the Shah ascended the Peacock Throne, ten when he survived the first attempt to assassinate him. Her family was deeply royalist and whenever the Shah appeared in the streets she would wait for hours to catch a glimpse of him. 'Every time I saw him I wept with emotion,' she confessed. As a student she joined in girlish chatter about who would be his next queen after his divorce from the beautiful Soraya. One of her friends jokingly suggested she would be the perfect choice and teasingly sent her a postcard on which was written 'Farah Diba – Farah Pahlavi.' She kept it. That one day she would in fact become empress and the greatest love of his life seemed as unlikely as a tale from the *One Thousand and One Nights*. Yet that is what happened in one of the most fascinating royal love stories of modern times.

They first met when the thirty-nine-year-old Shah went on a private visit to Paris in the spring of 1958. One evening his

Ambassador arranged a reception at the Embassy so that Iranian students of outstanding merit could be introduced to their sovereign. Farah Diba was among them. The tall, graceful girl was studying at the School of Architecture and lived in the *cité universitaire*, making do with a modest allowance and having to budget like any other student. She came from a highly respected family and her grandfather had been Iranian minister at The Hague, but she had never been in His Imperial Majesty's presence before.

Once Farah knew she was among those to be presented, she could hardly sleep for excitement. She spent hours brushing her blue-black hair into a smooth chignon and trying to tame her curly fringe. She chose a demure suit in black, grey and white tweed, then at the last minute pinned a white camellia at the neck, outlined her eyes with a touch of pencil and put a little colour on her lips, something she would never have dared to do in Iran. She describes their meeting in her autobiography, *My Thousand and One Days*.

The Shah was in a corner of the big reception room at the Embassy and the students filed past him one by one. When it came to her turn she gazed into his stern, handsome face.

'What are you studying?' he asked.

'Architecture, Majesty.'

'Do you not think that rather unusual for a woman?'

She stammered some reply, and when he went on to ask if she found the French language difficult she explained she had already learned French in Teheran. That was all. Except that she noticed that his eyes were sad. When the other students pressed closely round to talk to him, she hung back. It seemed to her too presumptuous, too familiar. She went back to her student lodgings determined never to forget a moment of that wonderful evening. But in later years the Shah would tease her about the fact that he couldn't remember meeting her in Paris at all!

It was no wonder that a romantic, impressionable girl like Farah Diba should have been so mesmerized by Mohammed Reza Pahlavi. In his prime he was a man of magnetic power, handsome with dark Middle Eastern features, athletic and strong. He gave an impression of a man who had iron control of himself and who could be equally ruthless with others. His family, however, knew that he could also be gentle and kind. Though he seldom revealed his innermost self, he obviously loved his country passionately.

He had been trained from the earliest age to conceal his emotions. As Crown Prince he had been subjected to the harshest discipline. His father, Reza Shah, was a fearsome man. 'He had only to fix his piercing eyes on us and we went rigid with fear and respect,' he told Margaret Laing in a rare inverview. At the age of six he was separated from his mother in order to be educated for his future role as Shah. His father became the greatest influence in his life. From the age of six the Crown Prince spent one hour each day with Reza Shah. From the age of nine he lunched daily with him, always eating the same thing, boiled chicken and rice. It was more of an ordeal than a pleasure for the little prince.

As he grew older the affairs of state were gradually introduced to him. But Reza Shah, for all his tyranny, realized that Iran needed educated and enlightened rulers. It was a turbulent country with corruption rife among the aristocrats and revolution stirring among the largely illiterate peasants. He wanted his son to learn the ways of the West and sent him to Switzerland to be educated. The experience was a mixed blessing as the Crown Prince was not allowed to have the same freedom as other pupils and had to submit to a regime dictated from Teheran. Nevertheless, he returned to his own country at the age of sixteen full of new ideas and convinced that his father's method of ruling by fear was wrong. He was determined that when his time came he would bring in democracy with 'firm discipline'. Iranians, he once said, were by nature unruly, and without discipline descended into anarchy.

Arranged marriages were the accepted form in Iran, as in other Middle Eastern countries, and Reza Shah was intent on finding a bride for his son who would bring with her considerable financial and political advantages. One day the Crown Prince was told that he had been betrothed to Princess Fawzia of Egypt. The arrangement was sudden even by Middle East standards. The Crown Prince had never set eyes on her and had not even been told that plans were being made on his behalf. Fawzia, however, was so lovely that his heart melted and after their marriage on 15 March 1939 they were hardly ever apart. The Princess had also been educated in Switzerland and was a comparatively modern girl who had never worn the veil. The Crown Prince was obviously delighted with her, but after a year the honeymoon was over and cracks in the marriage began to show.

For one thing, Princess Fawzia was expected to obey her father-in-law, the Shah, and the Empress Tadj-ol-Molouk, who was a formidable lady in her own right, but the Egyptian princess came from a wealthy, powerful court and was used to having her own way. The problems of a poor country like Iran were of no interest to her. She refused to share her young husband's burdens of state, complained about the climate and generally made it known that she was bored and dissatisfied. After the first year of marriage the two began to lead separate lives in separate apartments. The happiest outcome of the union was the birth of their daughter, Shahnaz, in 1940.

When both Britian and Russia invaded Iran during the Second World War, Reza Shah decided to abdicate, go into exile and leave his son to clear up the mess. The new King of Kings was three weeks short of his twenty-second birthday and, though outwardly cool and in control, was understandably furious at being pitched on to the throne with so little ceremony and at such a difficult time. At the end of the War, when the Allies left and the Iranian dust settled, Fawzia announced that she had decided to return to her native Egypt, taking her daughter with her. They were divorced on 19 November 1948 and the Shah did not see his child again for five years.

Now twenty-nine, the young King took his duties seriously but also followed the pursuits of any healthy sporting man, riding, swimming, sailing and relaxing occasionally in a nightclub. He disdained the idea that he should have a bodyguard because he never thought he was in any danger. On 4 February 1949, visiting the University of Teheran for its annual commemoration, he was made to realize just how vulnerable he was. Four shots were fired by an assassin. One bullet passed through his cheekbone and came out under his nose. Three went right through his military cap without touching him. The gunman fired again, wounding him in the shoulder. They stood face to face for a second, the gun pointing at the Shah's heart, but his courage held and the assassin was overpowered.

Mohammed Reza's second marriage was to the stunning Soraya Esfandiari, an eighteen-year-old beauty with dark hair and green

180

eyes. She was not of pure Iranian blood – her mother was German – but her father was descended from a long line of chieftains of the great Bakhtiari tribe. There was a whirlwind courtship and they were married on 12 February 1951, a day which the Court astrologers picked as specially favourable for His Imperial Majesty.

The astrologers were wrong. Though the couple loved each other, the seven-year marriage was ill-fated from the start. Soon after their betrothal Soraya contracted typhoid and was only saved when the Shah's personal doctor sent to America for the new wonder-drug Aureomycin. She was still weak on the day of the wedding and as it was bitterly cold had to wear thick woollen underwear beneath her fabulous Dior gown. Their honeymoon had to be postponed because of the country's political troubles. Like Fawzia, Soraya soon realized that her mother-in-law was the power behind the throne. She found it was almost impossible to be alone with the Shah because almost every evening the entire Pahlavi family was present.

These were the years of the oil crisis in Iran, when the wily, ambitious Dr Mossadeq nationalized the British-owned oil industry and, seeking total power for himself, became the Shah's bitterest enemy. The battle between them led to a coup in August 1953. The Shah and Soraya fled to Iraq, then Rome, fearing that the Peacock Throne was lost for ever. There was, however, still strong support for the monarchy. Mossadeq was overthrown in a counter-coup and the royal couple returned to a rapturous welcome.

The young Shah had suffered terribly and from that time on trusted no one, but there was tragedy of a more personal nature to come. His only full blood brother, Ali Reza, was killed in a plane crash in the Elburtz mountains outside Teheran, leaving him without anyone he could name as his direct heir. After that he could not sleep at night. Soraya, to their great sorrow, had proved unable to have children. The Shah's ministers did not hide their concern. What use was a barren queen? What if something happened to him? Revolution or anarchy would be inevitable. He must have an heir.

Their dilemma was soon being discussed openly and though the Shah did all he could to protect Soraya's dignity and feelings, he was left in no doubt that it was his duty to divorce her and

181

find someone who could give him children. So in March 1958 she left for St Moritz and an unsatisfactory life among the jet-setting pleasure-seekers, and he broadcast his decision to the nation in a voice that shook with emotion.

Though he was urged to look for a new queen immediately, the Shah found himself unable to take much interest in the young women introduced to him. His aura of proud isolation increased. Now he really was a man who walked alone.

Two months after his divorce from Soraya he went on the private visit to Paris where he met, and seemingly forgot that he had met, a student called Farah Diba. Neither of them, as it turned out, realized the significance of that brief encounter.

Stories that Farah was a Cinderella figure from an impoverished background had no basis in fact. Though her mother was a widow and, as an overseas student, she had to count her francs, the family was comfortably off, and its ancestry could be traced back to The Prophet. The Dibas were landowners, country gentry from the province of Azerbaijan in the north-west, bordering on Turkey. Farah was born on 15 October 1938. Her father, a diplomat, died when she was only ten and her relationship with her mother, who was an ardent worker for health and social reform, became very close. Her name meant 'joy' in Persian and with her huge, dark eyes and sweet, forthright nature she lived up to it.

She was educated at some of the best schools in Iran, first the Italian School of Teheran, then the Jeanne d'Arc High School run by sisters of the Order of St Vincent de Paul. She learned to speak French fluently. Always a bit of a tomboy, she questioned why she couldn't do certain things and found it hard to keep within the strict Islamic rules for women. She was a vigorous captain of the basket-ball team.

When the time came for Farah to decide upon a career she startled everyone by choosing architecture. There were no women architects in Iran at that time but she argued that she wanted to do something creative and useful and she thought women *ought* to be involved in the planning of schools, hospitals and housing developments. She had a staunch ally in her uncle, Mohammed Ghotbi, himself an architect, who advised his niece to go to Paris and enrolled her at the Ecole Spéciale d'Architecture on the Boulevard Raspail.

Farah was thrilled by the magic of Paris and enjoyed every moment of her life there, besides working hard at her studies. She proved to be an outstanding student and a natural choice when it came to selecting a group of young Iranians to be presented to the Shah. Their brief moment together at the Embassy reception, the few words he spoke, lingered on in her memory.

In July 1959 Farah Diba retured to her home in Teheran for the holidays. Like all students at the Ecole she was expected to spend part of the vacation preparing an architectural study. She had chosen to concentrate on the mosque in Isfahan where she drew plans, sketched the mosaics and spent hours in the museum with her nose buried in dusty old books. She led a quiet life among her family and girl friends, not really expecting much to happen that summer.

Before going back to Paris to continue her studies she needed a further grant to pay her fees. Her uncle suggested that she went to see Ardeshir Zahedi, a young diplomat in Teheran whose job it was to deal with all questions arising from Iranian students studying at foreign universities. Zahedi was married to the Shah's daughter, Princess Shahnaz. He was so attracted by Farah's natural charm and graceful manner that he decided to present her to his wife. The three of them became good friends.

Princess Shahnaz knew that her father was a lonely man and that he was being urged to look for a wife. He had made it clear to his advisers, however, that nothing would make him rush into another marriage. This time his choice would have to be the right one. All the young beauties of Teheran had been paraded before him at various parties and receptions but his heart remained like a stone. Princess Shahnaz made up her mind to invite her father to dinner and introduce him to her new friend.

Nothing was said to Farah. She was simply invited to spend a few hours with the Princess. The Shah arrived without any ceremony, greeted his daughter affectionately and looked searchingly into the face of the tall, dark-haired girl being presented to him. 'I was very anxious and my heart was beating,' she wrote in her memoirs. She tried to behave naturally. 'I made no attempt to play the courtier…but I was no fool and when I saw the King arriving I realized I was there to see if I pleased him or not.'

He questioned her about her studies in Paris and asked how

she came to speak such fluent French. She reminded him that they had met once before. He could not recall the meeting, though he remembered the occasion. She had been only one of many students then but now he became aware of her as a very beautiful young woman.

They both recorded their reactions to that memorable evening. Farah wrote, 'The King asked me questions and was very kind. I was glad to discover that I was talking to an ordinary mortal for, when one is young, one imagines that kings and queens live differently, walk differently, have their being somewhere beyond the reach of ordinary mortals. But he was very approachable and very human.' As for the Shah, not only was he struck by her beauty but he was even more impressed by her natural manner – 'so charming, interested in everything, obviously with a mind of her own'. One quite trivial detail told him, he felt, something very important about her. They were playing quoits on the terrace and they were landing all over the place. It was Farah who, without any fuss, bent down and picked them up. 'I liked that, for it meant she was without affectation.'

They met a number of times afterwards at the house of Princess Shahnaz. He talked to her about her plans, about herself and his own life until he gained her confidence and gradually she began to lose the awe she had felt for him since childhood. Instead, she became aware of his magnetism as a man and realized she was falling under his spell. 'Every time I was to meet him, my heart beat fast at the thought of seeing him. I was very, very excited but as soon as I found myself once more in his presence, I became quite calm and natural again. I never tried to appear different, more intelligent, more elegant or more interesting. I remained as I always was.'

Her feminine intuition told her what was happening but she kept telling herself that it was all a dream. The Shah invited her to lunch with him at the palace and took her for a flight over the desert in his personal plane. Throughout the whole month of September 1959 Farah Diba was secretly courted by the Shah. He said nothing to his family or his ministers but in his own mind he was sure he had found his new empress.

One day they were at the house of Princess Shahnaz, sitting together on a small sofa in the drawing-room while other guests milled around them talking and laughing. Suddenly the room cleared and they were alone. Very gently the Shah reminded her that he had been married twice already and that both marriages had ended for reasons of state. Great pressure had been put upon him to find a new empress but he had waited until he knew in his heart and mind that he had found the one whom destiny had intended for him. In a low voice he asked if she would be willing to marry him. He had known from their first meeting that he wanted her to be his wife but, he added, eventually there would be heavy responsibilities and she would be expected to serve the country by his side.

There was only one answer Farah Diba could give him. She had always felt a strong emotion for him even before they met. Now, when it seemed he needed her, she did not hesitate. Deeply moved, she accepted his proposal. She was happy, proud, and excited and a little alarmed at what was happening to her. The following days passed like a dream. She was 'a little bit in the clouds' and could not fully realize how much her life would now change. She had never had a boyfriend of any importance but now felt overwhelming affection and love for a man twenty years older than herself.

Only those closest to them were told that the Shah had proposed and been accepted. Farah's mother, although proud, was also concerned for the happiness of her daughter, realizing that she was very young for the responsibilities that would inevitably fall upon her. Meeting the royal family and the formidable Tadj-ol-Molouk, her future mother-in-law, was the first test of her courage. The Pahlavis were a powerful, close-knit group but they immediately recognized the special quality of this girl. Though shy and somewhat nervous, she reminded herself that the Shah *had* asked for her hand in marriage, and in that lay her strength. He loved her and that was all that mattered. As it turned out, her natural, graceful conduct won over her mother-in-law from the very beginning. There had been difficulties with the Empress Soraya. Farah saw clearly enough that Tadj-ol-Molouk was a strong, tough, dominant personality but admired her and the way she spoke her mind frankly to everyone alike. There was immense relief when it was seen that the two women were obviously going to get on well together.

While speculation mounted in Teheran, Farah Diba flew back to Paris on 20 October, ostensibly to continue her third-year studies at the Ecole d'Architecture, but in fact to shop for her trousseau. The Shah had told her to buy twelve of everything she wanted and sent his sisters, the elegant and cosmopolitan Princesses Shams, Ashraf and Fatemeh to help with the transformation of Farah from student to Empress.

Only a few weeks before she had been living in a university hostel on the Left Bank, cramming all her belongings into a small room with a simple wooden bed and a wash-basin hidden in a cupboard. Now she was installed in a luxurious suite at the Crillon Hotel and people began to wonder who the slender, dark-eyed girl could be. Most of the top couturiers, hairdressers and jewellers were seen rushing in and out of her rooms carrying mysterious boxes and confections in clouds of tissue paper. Rumours began to fly around Paris. She had ordered a wedding dress from Dior and chosen a magnificent diamond cluster ring from one of the great jewellers in the Rue St Honoré. Though no official announcement had come from Teheran, the world's press discovered that former architecture student Madamoiselle Farah Diba was to be the Shah's bride. Photographers and reporters began to follow her around Paris. On her last night in the capital she went to the Opéra, her blue-black hair sleekly coiffeured, her bejewelled evening dress worn with a white mink cape. Though President and Madame de Gaulle were present, the attention of the whole house was turned upon this beautifully dressed, quiet, composed girl.

She returned to Teheran at the beginning of November and, though the engagement had still not been officially announced, Court officials gathered at the airport to greet her. Their eyes opened wide when they saw descending the steps from the aircraft a poised, elegant young woman who received their bouquets with natural grace. Farah Diba had already stepped into her new role.

They were officially betrothed at a ceremony at the palace attended by members of both families, a few ministers and some courtiers. It was quite simple. Farah wore a sea-green dress, heavily embroidered, but no jewels. The Shah, a handsome, smiling figure in bemedalled Airforce uniform, gave her a ring and they celebrated with tea and cakes. On 23 November the official announcement was made, setting the wedding date for 21 December, two months after Farah's twenty-first birthday, and from that moment the telephones of the international press were kept busy night and day. No detail was too trivial to be recorded. Going over the top in their efforts to present her as an ordinary girl, some newspapers described her as an Iranian shepherdess, others as a Cinderella figure. This irritated and annoyed her family with its historic and important ties!

The month before they were married was very precious to the Shah and his bride-to-be. Once the affairs of state began to hem them in, there were only a few occasions when they could enjoy such freedom together. The two of them lunched alone each day. They went for long drives through the countryside, rode together and sometimes went up in the Shah's private plane. 'It was a very small plane which tossed considerably in the slightest wind,' she noted in her autobiography. 'One day the undercarriage would not come down. Below on the airfield I could see numbers of ambulances and fire engines. We were alone together in the plane and the King asked me to take a crank handle to try to dislodge the wheels. Fortunately, it all ended well.'

Teheran was under a thick mantle of snow for the day of the wedding, which was held in the glittering Hall of Reception at the Marble Palace, where walls and ceiling of cut-glass mirrored thousands of lights. In the icy dusk of a winter afternoon Farah Diba was a dazzling figure as she walked beneath the Koran, held symbolically above her head, and took her place by the side of the Shah. Her Dior gown with its billowing skirts was thickly embroidered with jewels and pearls; her veil was held in place by one of the great set pieces of the Crown jewels, a diamond coronet with an enormous rose diamond in the centre. Fabulous diamonds and emeralds blazed round her neck and in her ears. As she entered with six small girls in filmy white carrying her train and a small boy walking in front of her scattering white flowers, she looked like every child's idea of a story-book queen.

According to tradition, the couple sat before a low wedding table on which were displayed a number of symbolic objects. There was a mirror to symbolize happiness, candles to symbolize light, a sugar loaf to represent sweetness, gold for wealth, incense, the Koran, a goblet of clear water and some cakes. The mullah recited prayers from the Koran, then began the ritual of asking the bride three times if she was willing to wed. By tradition she should remain silent until the third time of asking but Farah was so excited she said 'Yes' the first time. Then, when it came to the exchanging of rings, she realized she had not bought one to give her husband. In a moment of smiling confusion they borrowed one from the Shah's son-in-law as a temporary measure. That evening the new Empress presided at a great banquet at the Golestan Palace, a picture of radiant happiness beside a Shah obviously in love. To end the day she was handed a cage full of turtle doves, which she set free as a token of happiness and peace.

Plans for a honeymoon in the sun had to be postponed. They spent a few days by the Caspian Sea, then returned to Teheran. The euphoria of that brilliant wedding day was short lived, for political troubles of all kinds were waiting. It was not an easy time for a twenty-one-year-old girl to become Empress. Iran was a vast, under-developed country with a population scattered over a barren and often mountainous terrain. The Shah's main ambition was to turn it into a stable, modern state, but he had many powerful enemies, among them the religious leader Ayatollah Khomeini and rich landlords who did not want change. Great progress had been made since the Mossadeq era, for Iran was beginning to reap the benefits of running her own oil industry. There had been significant steps forward in both education and health. Opium addiction and malaria, which until 1950 had been two of the country's greatest health hazards, were virtually eliminated. New ports, dams, hospitals and colleges were the signs of an expanding nation.

The young Empress was full of idealism and soon made a favourable impression as she travelled about the country with the Shah. In the first year of her marriage she visited the Abadan Refineries in the Gulf and asked to see the workers' living conditions. What she was shown shocked her deeply. She burst into tears. Her deep concern for ordinary people was evident and she promised herself she would do what she could to help.

Farah knew, however, that her first priority was to produce an heir for the Peacock Throne. To her relief she became pregnant two months after the wedding. The birth of a fine healthy boy, named Reza after his grandfather, was received with an outburst of joy throughout Iran. The birth was not easy but when she recovered consciousness the Shah was holding her hand.

'Do you know what it is?'

'Tell me,' she murmured.

'It's a boy.'

She burst into tears. 'My God,' she wrote in her memoirs, 'what if it had been a girl? Everyone would have been so disappointed.' The Shah proclaimed holidays for the whole of Iran, a twenty per cent reduction in tax and an amnesty for ninety-eight prisoners. Three more children were born to them over the next decade: their daughter Farahnaz in 1963, another son, Ali Reza, named after the Shah's brother, in 1966 and their second daughter, Leila, in 1970. Family life was happy and content, never more so than when they were able to escape from Teheran to a simple house by the Caspian Sea where they would swim, ride and play ball games on the beach with the children.

As soon as she was able Farah began the work she was longing to do. She gave her time and energy to a host of social problems, concerning herself with anything that would improve the lot of ordinary people, especially women and children. This included visiting Iran's leper colony. Soon she was working eight hours a day, with a staff of forty, not counting official dinners and receptions. 'She works too hard, too hard,' the Shah would tell people. Outwardly elegant, the epitome of *chic*, inwardly she was a very warm and sensitive woman.

But in spite of her efforts and the Shah's attempts to bring about reform by means of his 'White Revolution', the period after their marriage was disturbed. The early Sixties saw riots in the universities and among the powerful mullahs, the religious leaders led by Khomeini, who did not like the idea of land reform or the prospect of votes for women. The troublesome Khomeini was eventually sent into exile in November 1963.

Two years later, on 10 April 1965, there was a second attempt on the Shah's life when a twenty-two-year-old soldier doing his military service with the Imperial Guard went berserk with a machine-gun. As he advanced towards the Shah's office in the Marble Palace, firing wildly, he was shot down, but not before killing two of the royal bodyguards. A bullet penetrated the door but the Shah did not even move from his desk. It was, he said, the will of God. Farah said that when she heard the news her heart stopped beating. The shock had a curious effect. Once she knew her husband was safe she continued putting on her make-up chanting, 'Thank you, God. Thank you, God.'

189

It was not until 1967, when he had been on the throne for twenty-six years, that the Shah decided the time had come for his coronation. He had always said that he did not wish to be consecrated king of a poverty-stricken people, but now that certain reforms had brought about a better standard of living and more hope for the future he decided to go ahead with the ceremony. It was an occasion of Byzantine magnificence. When planning it the Shah had said, 'This, the most important day of my life, shall be the greatest day of her life, too.' Having first placed the high, jewel-encrusted Pahlavi crown on his own head, he turned and gently set the specially designed crown of emeralds, rubies and pearls on the sleek dark hair of his Empress, his Shahbanou. As Lesley Blanch says in her biography of Farah, 'With this crowning he invested her with the powers of Regent. Never had the wife of a Persian ruler been accorded such an honour. It was seen as a revolutionary measure of profound significance throughout Islam where in general women are still relegated to the background and the four walls of their own homes.' Whatever it meant to the outside world, to the Shah it was obviously a gesture of love for his wife.

Perhaps the gesture had been too revolutionary. Iran's roots were deep in Islam. The Shah's attempts through the Sixties to bring about reforms through democracy had been opposed all along by the mullahs and great landowners. He dreamed of Iran being a great modern civilization but his dream was beginning to turn sour. Advances had been made but now betrayals and further plots against him frustrated every move. Abandoning democracy, he decided to rule by decree.

During the Seventies the world saw a Shah becoming more like his father in his use of absolute authority and his retreat into isolation. To the outside world the land of roses and nightingales did not always present a pleasant face. The state security and intelligence agency SAVAK, seemingly a power unto itself, became notorious as a brutal secret police. The face of the Empress became tired and strained.

Thirteen years had passed since the Shah had deported the Ayatollah Khomeini. The deadly priest had become a martyr. As Iran descended into ever greater confusion, from Paris he master-minded a crippling general strike and cried, 'The Pahlavi dynasty must go.' On his fifty-ninth birthday the Shah freed 1,126

190

political prisoners but in the streets frenzied crowds called for his death. Khomeini urged them to shed 'rivers of blood' to overthrow his enemy.

After a year of turmoil, thousands of deaths and frenetic hatred, the Ayatollah won. The Shah saw there would be no end to it all until he fled from Iran. Members of his family had already gone, accusations of corruption and avarice hurled after them. He had sent his children to safety in America. There remained only Farah and himself.

On 16 January 1978 the Shah and his Empress were driven to the aiport. There were emotional scenes as the faithful said their farewells. The Shah himself had tears in his eyes as he said stiffly, 'I hope the government will be able to make amends for the past and also succeed in laying a foundation for the future.' He bent and raised a member of the Iranian guard who tried to kiss his feet. Someone handed him a packet of Iranian soil, then, taking Farah gently by the arm, he led her to the waiting plane. At the controls of the Boeing 707 he flew with her into exile.

Their last days together were tragic and almost friendless. For political reasons no country seemed willing to give the Shah and his family sanctuary for longer than a few months at a time. They were moved on from five countries in eighteen months and with each move the Shah's health deteriorated. Eventually it was the courageous President Sadat of Egypt, himself one day to be the victim of an assassin's bullet, who offered him asylum. Sadat gave orders that two floors of a military hospital were to be sealed off and prepared to receive the Shah and it was there he died in the last days of July 1980, a stricken Empress Farah by his bedside hardly comprehending what had happened.

President Sadat ordered a full state funeral for the Shah and sent Egyptian air force jets to fly past in tribute. The funeral took place on a blistering hot day but Farah and the Shah's sister Ashraf were in black from head to foot, their black lace veils falling almost to the ground. They walked for over a mile behind the coffin which was covered with an Iranian flag and drawn on a gun-carriage by six black horses. Crown Prince Reza walked proudly beside his mother. Only two of the Shah's friends from his days of splendour bothered to come; one was ex-King Constantine of Greece, himself an exile, and the other was former President Nixon of the United States.

When the procession reached the Rifale Mosque, Farah and the other women were led to a tent while the men went inside to say prayers. Farah was almost overcome and had to be supported while Ashraf collapsed into the arms of Madame Sadat. Inside the mosque a priest chanted over the coffin, 'Merciful God, forgive his soul for anything he has done wrong.' Farah still could not understand why all those who had wooed her husband when he was in power ignored him in exile. Broken-hearted, she turned away from the great tomb where her husband had been laid to rest with kings of Egypt and, her eyes full of tears, walked alone into the heat of the Egyptian day.